High School

ASSESSMENT PACKAGE

1

BERKELEY
HARVARD
MICHIGAN STATE
SHELL CENTRE

Balanced Assessment for the
Mathematics Curriculum

Dale Seymour Publications®

Project Directors: Alan Schoenfeld
                       Hugh Burkhardt
                       Phil Daro
                       Jim Ridgway
                       Judah Schwartz
                       Sandra Wilcox

Managing Editors: Alan MacDonell and Catherine Anderson

Acquisitions Editor: Merle Silverman

Project Editor: Toni-Ann Guadagnoli

Production/Manufacturing Director: Janet Yearian

Senior Production/Manufacturing Coordinator: Fiona Santoianni

Design Director: Phyllis Aycock

Design Manager: Jeff Kelly

Cover and Interior Designer: Don Taka

Cover Image: Hutchings Photography

Illustrator: Elizabeth Allen

The work of this project was supported by a grant from the National Science Foundation.
The opinions expressed in these materials do not necessarily represent the position, policy,
or endorsement of the Foundation.

This book is published by Dale Seymour Publications®,
an imprint of Addison Wesley Longman, Inc.

Dale Seymour Publications
10 Bank Street
White Plains, NY 10602-5026
Customer Service: 800-872-1100

Printed in the United States of America
Order number 33006
ISBN 0-7690-0069-X

2 3 4 5 6 7 8 9 10-ML-02-01-00-99

This Book Is Printed
On Recycled Paper

This assessment package was designed and developed by members of the Balanced Assessment Project team, particularly Jana Branissa, Joanne Lobato, Susan Dean, Manuel Santos, Alan Schoenfeld, Ann Shannon, Dick Stanley, Malcolm Swan, Marion Walter, and Dan Zimmerlin. The editor was Ann Shannon.

Many others have made helpful comments and suggestions in the course of the development. We thank them all. The project is particularly grateful to the administrators, teachers, and students with whom these tasks were developed and tested.

The project was directed by Alan Schoenfeld, Hugh Burkhardt, Phil Daro, Jim Ridgway, Judah Schwartz, and Sandra Wilcox.

The package consists of materials compiled or adapted from work done at the four sites of the Balanced Assessment Project:

Balanced Assessment
Graduate School of Education
University of California
Berkeley, CA 94720-1670
USA

Balanced Assessment (MARS)
513 Erickson Hall
Michigan State University
East Lansing, MI 48824
USA

Balanced Assessment
Educational Technology Center
Harvard University
Cambridge, MA 02138
USA

Balanced Assessment
Shell Centre for Mathematical
Education
University of Nottingham
Nottingham NG7 2RD
England

Additional tasks and packages, the materials in their original form, and other assessment resources such as guides to scoring may be obtained from the project sites. For a full list of available publications, and for further information, contact the Project's Mathematics Assessment Resource Service (MARS) at the Michigan State address above. We welcome your comments.

Table of Contents

What is balanced assessment?

Mathematics assessments tell us and our students how well they are learning mathematics. A carefully designed mathematics assessment should:

- assess the mathematics that counts, focusing on important ideas and processes;

- be fair to the students, providing them with a set of opportunities to demonstrate what they know and can do;

- be fair to the curriculum, offering a balance of opportunities—long and short tasks, basic knowledge and problem solving, individual and group work, and the spectrum of concepts and processes that reflect the vision of the NCTM *Standards;*

- be of such high quality that students and teachers learn from them—so that assessment time serves as instructional time, and assessment and curriculum live in harmony;

- provide useful information to administrators, so they can judge the effectiveness of their programs; to teachers, so they can judge the quality of their instruction; and to students and parents, so they can see where the students are doing well and where more work is needed.

This is such an assessment package, dealing with the mathematics appropriate for the high school students. It was designed by the Balanced Assessment Project, an NSF-supported collaboration that was funded to create a series of exemplary assessment items and packages for assessing students' mathematical performance at various grade levels (elementary grades, middle grades, high school, and advanced high school). Balanced Assessment offers a wide range of extensively field-tested tasks and packages—some paper-and-pencil, some high-tech or multimedia—and consulting services to help states and districts implement meaningful and informative mathematics assessments.

What is balance?

It's easy to see what isn't balanced. An assessment that focuses on computation only is out of balance. So is one that focuses on patterns, functions, and algebra to the exclusion of geometry, shape, and space, or that ignores or gives a cursory nod toward statistics and probability. Likewise, assessments that do not provide students with ample opportunity to show how they can reason or communicate mathematically are unbalanced. These are content and process dimensions of balance, but there are many others—length of task, whether tasks are pure or applied, and so on. The following table shows some of the dimensions used to design and balance this package.
(For explanations of terms that may be unfamiliar, see the Glossary.)

Dimensions of Balance

Mathematical Content Dimension

- **Mathematical Content** will include some of the following:

  Number and Quantity including: concepts and representation; computation; estimation and measurement; number theory and general number properties.

  Patterns, Functions, and Algebra including: patterns and generalization; functional relationships (including ratio and proportion); graphical and tabular representation; symbolic representation; forming and solving relationships.

  Geometry, Shape, and Space including: shape, properties of shapes, relationships; spatial representation, visualization, and construction; location and movement; transformation and symmetry; trigonometry.

  Handling Data, Statistics, and Probability including: collecting, representing, and interpreting data; probability models—experimental and theoretical; simulation.

  Other Mathematics including: discrete mathematics, including combinatorics; underpinnings of calculus; mathematical structures.

Mathematical Process Dimension

- **Phases** of problem solving, reasoning, and communication will include, as broad categories, some or all of the following: modeling and formulating; transforming and manipulating; inferring and drawing conclusions; checking and evaluating; reporting.

Task Type Dimensions

- **Task Type** will be one of the following: open investigation; nonroutine problem; design; plan; evaluation and recommendation; review and critique; re-presentation of information; technical exercise; definition of concepts.

- **Nonroutineness** in: context; mathematical aspects or results; mathematical connections.

- **Openness:** It may have an open end with open questions; open middle.

- **Type of Goal** is one of the following: pure mathematics; illustrative application of the mathematics; applied power over the practical situation.

- **Reasoning Length** is the expected time for the longest section of the task. (It is an indication of the amount of "scaffolding"—the detailed step-by-step guidance that the prompt may provide.)

Circumstances of Performance Dimensions

- **Task Length:** ranging from short tasks (5–15 minutes), through long tasks (45–60 minutes), to extended tasks (several days to several weeks).

- **Modes of Presentation:** written; oral; video; computer.

- **Modes of Working** on the task: individual; group; mixed.

- **Modes of Response** by the student: written; built; spoken; programmed; performed.

What's in a package?

A typical Balanced Assessment Package offers ten to twenty tasks, ranging in length from 5 to 45 minutes. Some of the tasks consist of a single problem, while others consist of a sequence of problems. Taken together, the tasks provide students with an opportunity to display their knowledge and skills across the broad spectrum of content and processes described in the NCTM *Standards*. It takes time to get this kind of rich information—but the problems are mathematically rich and well worth the time spent on them.

What's included with each task?

We have tried to provide you with as much information as possible about the mathematics central to solving a task, about managing the assessment, and about typical student responses and how to analyze the mathematics in them. Each section of this package, corresponding to one task, consists of the following:

Overview   The first page of each section provides a quick overview that lets you see whether the task is appropriate for use at any particular point in the curriculum. This overview includes the following:

- Task Description—the situation that students will be asked to investigate or solve.

- Assumed Mathematical Background—the kinds of previous experiences students will need to have had to engage the task productively.

- Core Elements of Performance—the mathematical ideas and processes that will be central to the task.

- Circumstances—the estimated time for students to work on the task; the special materials that the task will require; whether students will work individually, in pairs or in small groups; and any other such information.

Task Prompt   These pages are intended for the student. To make them easy to find, they have been designed with stars in the margin and a white bar across the top. The task prompt begins with a statement for the student characterizing the aims of the task. In some cases there is a pre-assessment activity that teachers assign in advance of the formal assessment. In some cases there is a launch activity that familiarizes students with the context but is not part of the formal assessment.

Sample Solution   Each task is accompanied by at least one solution; where there are multiple approaches to a problem, more than one may appear.

Using this Task   Here we provide suggestions about launching the task and helping students understand the context of the problem. Some tasks have pre-activities; some have students do some initial exploration in pairs or as a whole class to become familiar with the context while the formal assessment is done individually. Information from field-testing about aspects of tasks that students may find challenging is given here. We may also include suggestions for subsequent classroom instruction related to the task, as well as possible extensions that can be used for assessment or instructional purposes.

Characterizing Performance   This section contains descriptions of characteristic student responses that the task is likely to elicit. These descriptions, based on the *Core Elements of Performance*, indicate various levels of successful engagement with the task. They are accompanied by annotated artists' renderings of typical student work. These illustrations of student work will prepare you to assess the wide range of responses produced by your students. We have chosen examples that show something of the range and variety of responses to the task, and the various aspects of mathematical performance it calls for. The commentary is intended to exemplify these key aspects of performance at various levels across several domains. Teachers and others have found both the examples and the commentary extremely useful; its purpose is to bring out explicitly for each task the wide range of aspects of mathematical performance that the standards imply.

Scoring student work

The discussions of student work in the section *Characterizing Performance* are deliberately qualitative and holistic, avoiding too much detail. They are designed to focus on the mathematical ideas that "count," summarized in the *Core Elements of Performance* for each task. They offer a guide to help teachers and students look in some depth at a student's work in the course of instruction, considering how it might be improved.

For some other purposes, we need more. Formal assessment, particularly if the results are used for life-critical decisions, demands more accurate scoring, applied consistently across different scorers. This needs more precise rubrics, linked to a clear scheme for reporting on performance. These can be in a variety of styles, each of which has different strengths. The Balanced Assessment Project has developed resources that support a range of styles.

For example, *holistic approaches* require the scorer to take a balanced overall view of the student's response, relating general criteria of quality in performance to the specific item. *Point scoring approaches* draw attention in detail to the various aspects of performance that the task involves, provide a natural mechanism for balancing greater strength in one aspect with some weakness in another, and are useful for *aggregating scores*.

How to use this package

This assessment package may be used in a variety of ways, depending on your local needs and circumstances.

- You may want to implement formal performance assessment under controlled conditions at the school, district, or state level. This package provides a balanced set of tasks appropriate for such on-demand, high-stakes assessment.

- You may want to provide opportunities for classroom-based performance assessment, embedded within the curriculum, under less controlled conditions. This package allows you the discretion of selecting tasks that are appropriate for use at particular points in the curriculum.

- You may be looking for tasks to serve as a transition toward a curriculum as envisioned in the NCTM *Standards* or as enrichment for existing curriculum. In this case, the tasks in this package can serve as rich instructional problems to enhance your curriculum. They are exemplars of the kinds of instructional tasks that will support performance assessment and can be used for preparing students for future performance assessment. Even in these situations, the tasks provide you with rich sites to engage in informal assessment of student understanding.

Preparing for the assessment

We urge you to work through a task yourself before giving it to your students. This gives you an opportunity to become familiar with the context and the mathematical demands of the task, and to anticipate what might need to be highlighted in launching the task.

It is important to have at hand all the necessary materials students need to engage a task before launching them on the task. We assume that students have certain tools and materials available at all times in the mathematics classroom and that these will be accessible to students to choose from during any assessment activity.

At the high school level these resources include: grid paper; dice, square tiles, cubes, and other concrete materials; calculators; rulers, compasses, and protractors or angle rulers; scissors, markers, tape, string, paper clips, and glue.

If a task requires any special materials, these are specified in the task.

Managing the assessment

We anticipate that this package will be used in a variety of situations. Therefore, our guidance about managing assessment is couched in fairly general suggestions. We point out some considerations you may want to take into account under various circumstances.

The way in which any particular task is introduced to students will vary. The launch will be shaped by a number of considerations (for example, the students, the complexity of the instructions, the degree of familiarity students have with the context of the problem). In some cases it will be necessary only to distribute the task to students and then let them read and work through the task. Other situations may call for you to read the task to the class to assure that everyone understands the instructions, the context, and the aim of the assessment. Decisions of this kind will be influenced by the ages of the students, their experiences with reading mathematical tasks, their fluency with English, and whether difficulties in reading would exclude them from otherwise productively engaging with the mathematics of the task.

Under conditions of formal assessment, once students have been set to work on a task, you should not intervene except where specified. This is essential in formal, high-stakes assessment but it is important under any assessment circumstance. Even the slightest intervention by you—reinterpreting instructions, suggesting ways to begin, offering prompts when students appear to be stuck—has the potential to alter the task for the student significantly. However, you should provide general encouragement within a supportive classroom environment as a normal part of doing mathematics in school. This includes reminding students about the aim of the assessment (using the words at the beginning of the task prompt), when the period of assessment is nearing an end, and how to turn in their work when they have completed the task.

We suggest a far more relaxed use of the package when students are meeting these kinds of tasks for the first time, particularly in situations where they are being used primarily as learning tasks to enhance the curriculum. Under these circumstances you may reasonably decide to do some coaching, talk with students as they work on a task, and pose questions when they seem to get stuck. In these instances you may be using the tasks for informal assessment—observing what strategies students favor, what kinds of questions they ask, what they seem to understand and what they are struggling with, what kinds of prompts get them unstuck. This can be extremely useful information in helping you make ongoing instructional and assessment decisions. However, as students have more experiences with these kinds of tasks, the amount of coaching you do should decline and students should rely less on this kind of assistance.

Under conditions of formal assessment, you will need to make decisions about how tasks will be scored and by whom, how scores will be aggregated across tasks, and how students' accomplishments will be reported to interested constituencies. These decisions will, of necessity, be made at the school, district, or state level and will likely reflect educational, political, and economic considerations specific to the local context.

Expanded Table of Contents*

Long Tasks	Task Type	Circumstances of Performance
1. Strange but True	45-minute problem illustrating an application of the mathematics in a nonroutine context from student life	individual written response after a whole-class introduction
2. Supermarket Carts	45-minute problem illustrating an application of the mathematics; it is a nonroutine context from adult life; an approach to the task is to be formulated	individual written response after a whole-class introduction
3. Assessing Logo Design	45-minute task involving an illustrative application of mathematics in a nonroutine context from adult life	individual written response
4. Designing a Staircase	45-minute design task involving applied power over a nonroutine context from adult life; open-ended	individual written response
5. Packaging a Soda Bottle	60-minute design task, applied power; nonroutine mathematical connections; adult-life context	individual written response after a discussion in pairs
6. Wheelchair Access	45-minute design task, applied power in a nonroutine context from student life; open-ended	individual written response
7. Kidney Stones	45-minute exercise; adult-life context; applied power	individual written response after a discussion in pairs

* For explanations of terms that may be unfamiliar, see the Glossary, and the *Dimensions of Balance* table in the Introduction

Mathematical Content	Mathematical Processes
Number and Quantity: involving mainly estimation and associated computation	formulation of the problem and interpretation of the results roughly match the manipulation demands of the computation
Number and Quantity: structural analysis, leads into algebra, formulating functional relationships in symbolic form	formulation of the approach selection of a numerical or structural approach, manipulation and transformation of numerical and algebraic forms
Functions in a geometric context: involving both specific and general formulation of linear and quadratic relationships arising from scaling transformations	interpretation and evaluation of the given student responses leads to formulation of appropriate reasoning; some associated manipulation
Geometry: involves mainly estimation and computation of number and quantity in finding solutions that satisfy three constraints, one of which is the slope	balance of formulation of the approach, manipulation, interpretation of the trial results and their evaluation; strategy involves conjecture and check
Geometry, Space, and Shape, with Number: visualization of the form of the net for cuboid and hexagonal prism boxes; measurement of given figure; computation with Pythagorean theorem	formulation of the approach; manipulation through measurement, calculation, and sketching
Geometry, Space, and Shape, with Number: visualization of forms for the ramp; computation of slope constraints	formulation of possible designs; transformation of constraints into dimensions; communication about the design and how it meets the conditions
Data, Statistics, and Probability: combining probabilities by addition and multiplication, with circle chart	manipulation and interpretation of the data given, formulation of the standard method for combining probabilities

Expanded Table of Contents

Short Tasks	Task Type	Circumstances of Performance
8. Lightning	15-minute problem involving applied power over a nonroutine context related to student life; tightly structured	individual written response
9. Homework, TV, and Sleep	15-minute exercise in a context from student life	individual written response
10. Wooden Water Tanks	15-minute problem involving applied power in a context from adult life	individual written response
11. Where's the Misprint?	15-minute problem involving applied power in a nonroutine context from adult life	individual written response
12. The Knockout	15-minute exercise; an illustrative application of probability	individual written response
13. Shadows	15-minute problem involving an illustrative application in a nonroutine context from student life	individual written response
14. Something's Fishy	15-minute task to prepare advice; applied power from nonroutine math in a context from adult life	individual written response
15. Miles of Words	15-minute problem involving an illustrative application in a nonroutine context from adult life	individual written response

Mathematical Content	Mathematical Processes
Number and Quantity: a geometric problem involving location from a nonroutine coordinate representation	transformation and manipulation is the main load, with some interpretation of information given or calculated; almost an exercise
Handling scatter plot data	interpretation and formulation of scatter plot data, with associated manipulation
Number and Quantity applied to the volume of a cylinder of given dimensions, embraces measurement	formulation and consequent transformation of the expressions
Number: recognizing and correcting mismatched proportions of votes	evaluation of information provided and formulation of possible corrections, with associated manipulation
Combining probabilities	manipulation of probability computations
Function in a geometric context: involving graphical and algebraic representation of relationships in similar triangles	formulation and transformation of the relationships involved
Data, Statistics, and Probability: capture-recapture models for estimating populations	formulation and manipulation of the models, together with communication of results in a report
Creation, estimation, and application of a rate	interpretation, formulation, and manipulation are evenly balanced

Strange but True

Interpret and make deductions from a piece of text.

Handle large numbers.

Develop an organized approach to problem solving.

Make reasonable assumptions and estimations.

Long Task

Task Description

This task presents a story about a woman who decided to write down every number from one to one million. Students are asked to interpret and make deductions from the article.

The task involves checking the number of digits the woman wrote; estimating the time she must have spent writing them each day; and calculating the distance that all these digits would stretch if they were laid end to end.

Assumed Mathematical Background

At a minimum, students should have had some experience using a calculator to manipulate large numbers. Also, it would be useful to know what is meant by the term *digit*.

Core Elements of Performance

- interpret data from a piece of written text
- use these data to solve problems and check solutions
- organize a systematic approach to a complex problem
- make sensible assumptions and estimates, and give answers to a reasonable degree of accuracy

Circumstances

Grouping:	Following a whole class introduction, students complete an individual written response.
Materials:	calculator
Estimated time:	45 minutes

Strange but True

This problem gives you the chance to

- *interpret data from a piece of text*
- *organize a systematic approach to a complex problem*
- *make sensible assumptions and estimates*
- *give answers to a reasonable degree of accuracy*

Sophia has the strangest obsession with numbers. Over the last two years, she has written out all the numbers from one to one million.

To reach the magical figure of 1 million, she filled forty workbooks. Each book contained 96 pages.

She wrote the numbers in 10 columns on each page. There were 26 numbers in each column.

She used 98 ball point pens.

The total number of single digits that Sophia has written is 5,888,896.

1. How many numbers did Sophia write on each page of her exercise books? Answer this question using two different methods if you can. Describe your two methods clearly.

2. Show how the figure 5,888,896 was obtained. Describe your method and show your work in an organized way.

3. Sophia took about one second to write down each digit. Suppose Sophia spread her work out evenly across the two years. About how long did she spend writing down numbers each day?

4. If all the numbers that Sophia wrote were laid end to end, how far would they stretch? Describe your reasoning and state any assumptions you make.

A Sample Solution

1. (i) Sophia wrote the numbers in 10 columns with 26 numbers in each column. This means she wrote 10 × 26 = 260 numbers per page.

   (ii) Sophia wrote 1 million numbers in forty 96-page books. She therefore wrote 1,000,000 ÷ (40 × 96) numbers on each page. This gives 260.4 numbers per page. This confirms the earlier calculation.

   (In fact, she would have completed exactly 40 books, 6 pages, 1 column, and 14 numbers in the second column.)

2.

Range	No. of digits per number	No. of numbers in range	No. of digits in range
1 – 9	1	9	9
10 – 99	2	90	180
100 – 999	3	900	2,700
1,000 – 9,999	4	9,000	36,000
10,000 – 99,999	5	90,000	450,000
100,000 – 999,999	6	900,000	5,400,000
1,000,000	7	1	7
		Total	5,888,896

3. $5{,}888{,}896 \text{ digits} \times \frac{1 \text{ sec}}{1 \text{ digit}} \times \frac{1 \text{ min}}{60 \text{ sec}} \times \frac{1 \text{ hour}}{60 \text{ min}} \approx 1636 \text{ hours.}$

   Spread over two years this amounts to $\frac{1636 \text{ hr}}{2 \text{ yr}} \times \frac{1 \text{ yr}}{365 \text{ days}} \approx 2.24 \text{ hrs/day.}$

4. Assume that there are about 4 digits per centimeter.

   Then $5{,}888{,}896 \text{ digits} \times \frac{1 \text{ cm}}{4 \text{ digits}} \times \frac{1 \text{ m}}{100 \text{ cm}} \approx 14{,}722 \text{ m.}$

   This assumes that there are no spaces between the numbers. We would expect students to allow for this and give their result to an appropriate degree of accuracy.

Task 1   **Using this Task**

If you are using this task as part of a formal system of assessment, it should be presented to students with standardized instructions. For such purposes, read through the text with the class. Illustrate the difference between *numbers* and *digits* by writing numbers 1 to 15 vertically on the board. Then stop and ask:

"How many numbers have I written so far?" (15)
"How many digits have I written so far?" (21)

Explain that Sophia went on to write all the numbers like this from one to one million.

Extensions

You may wish to extend this task by using some of the ideas that follow.

■ How long it would take to *read out* the numbers from one to one million? Some numbers take longer to say than others. We could count the syllables. Would it matter which language was used?

■ What does one million dollars look like? If a pile of one-dollar bills totaling one million dollars were made, how high would it be? Would the bills fit in a shopping bag?

Characterizing Performance

This section offers a characterization of student responses and provides indications of the ways in which the students were successful or unsuccessful in engaging with and completing the task. The descriptions are keyed to the *Core Elements of Performance*. Our global descriptions of student work range from "The student needs significant instruction" to "The student's work meets the essential demands of the task." Samples of student work that exemplify these descriptions of performance are included below, accompanied by commentary on central aspects of each student's response. These sample responses are *representative;* they may not mirror the global description of performance in all respects, being weaker in some and stronger in others.

The characterization of student responses for this task is based on these *Core Elements of Performance:*

1. Interpret data from a piece of written text.
2. Use these data to solve problems and check solutions.
3. Organize a systematic approach to a complex problem.
4. Make sensible assumptions and estimates, and give answers to a reasonable degree of accuracy.

Descriptions of Student Work

The student needs significant instruction.

These papers suggest that the student understands the text and can extract some relevant information from it.

Examples of this understanding would indicate that the student has located relevant information in the text for question 1 and has made some attempt to count the digits in question 2. The student has been unable to formulate or solve the problems in questions 3 and 4.

Student A

This response shows that the relevant information in question 1 is located and used correctly to calculate 260 numbers per page. It appears that no attempt is made to count the digits or create a systematic approach to question 2. There is a response in hours and minutes for question 3, but the response has failed to indicate how this was obtained. The student has also

Task

attempted a response to question 4 but does not state any assumptions that were made or provide any calculations to indicate how this conclusion was obtained.

The student needs some instruction.

These papers provide evidence that students can locate relevant information in text, make a sensible calculation, and solve a straightforward problem. The students remain unable to organize a systematic approach to a more complex problem, or make sensible assumptions and estimates, or give answers to a reasonable degree of accuracy.

In question 1, the student has located relevant information in the text and found one way of obtaining 260. The student has clearly understood the problem but has not been able to organize a suitable attack on it in question 2. In questions 3 and 4, the student has chosen some appropriate calculations to perform but may not have completed the problems, nor specified the answer to a sensible degree of accuracy.

Student B

This student has managed to answer question 1 by one method. The student has started to attempt question 2 by a systematic approach to counting the digits but crosses this work out and states that there is another method to do this but she doesn't know how to do it. In question 3, the student has misinterpreted the question and has solved (inaccurately) for the number of digits per day instead of the number of hours per day. The student makes an assumption for question 4 and raises several other questions that could be turned into assumptions, but she makes no attempt to solve the problem.

Student C

This student has correctly used the relevant information in question 1 to determine that there were 260 numbers per page, but he does not provide a second method. In question 2, the student makes an attempt to systematically determine the number of digits, but incorrectly counts the number in each grouping. The student provides a response to question 3 but does not indicate how this response was calculated. In question 4, the student gives a response but provides no reasoning or calculation to support it.

The student's work needs to be revised.

These papers provide evidence that students can locate relevant information in text, formulate an appropriate calculation, and solve a straightforward problem. They are also able to tackle a more complex task by first identifying a subproblem that is more manageable. Students make some sensible assumptions or estimates, though these may not be explicitly stated. Answers may not be given to a reasonable degree of accuracy.

The work shows that the student has used one or two ways of calculating 260. In question 2, some subtasks (but not all) have been identified and worked on. The student has counted digits for some ranges of the numbers, perhaps with minor calculation errors. The approach is appropriate and correct, but incomplete. In question 3, the student may have solved the problem almost completely and correctly, but may not have expressed the answer to a sensible degree of accuracy. Sensible assumptions have apparently been made in question 4, but these may not be stated explicitly. The reasoning is unclear or incomplete.

Student D

This student has answered question 1 by two methods. The student's response to question 2 is well organized and clearly presented. It is also correct, apart from one repeated error (the number of numbers in each range greater than 100 is miscalculated by one each time). The student has successfully calculated the time required per day. The student provides a response for question 4, but does not state any assumptions that were made or how the calculation was completed.

Student E

The student correctly solves question 1 by one method. The student shows a systematic approach to question 2 with correct calculations and a verbal description of his method. The student correctly calculates the number of hours spent each day. The student lists the assumptions that were used in question 4. The student's degree of accuracy is off due to the fact that he calculates the length of "boxes" laid end to end. This does not take into account that each box contains a different number of digits. There is no mention of spaces between numbers or boxes.

The student's work meets the essential demands of the task.

Almost all the core elements of performance are demonstrably present. The student has found one or two ways of solving question 1. The problem in question 2 has been broken down into clear subtasks; a table or other organized approach has been used. There may be a minor repeated calculation error (for example, assuming there are 89 numbers in range 10–99; 899 in range 100–999, etc.) but the method is appropriate, complete, and correct. The problem in question 3 has been correctly solved and the answer is presented to an appropriate degree of accuracy. Sensible assumptions have been made in question 4. The reasoning is clear and correct.

Task

Student F

The student correctly uses two different methods to solve question 1. The student work shows a systematic approach to question 2 as well as a correct response. The student also correctly solves for the correct number of hours per day. In question 4, the student makes an assumption about the width of each digit based upon measuring that she had done. The student then converts this measurement several times to end up with an answer in miles. No accounting of spaces is made.

Student G

This student explains two different methods for solving question 1 and both are executed correctly. The student also provides a written explanation for the systematic approach that was used to solve question 2. The student correctly solves for the number of hours in question 3. In question 4, the student makes an assumption as to the width of each digit and then performs the necessary calculations. The student's response is indicated in millimeters and kilometers, but steps for this process are not indicated.

Student A

1) You get 10 Multiply it by 26 to get 260
10 Represent 10 Columns 26 Represents 26 numbers
In a Column.

2)

3) 8 Hours & 28 Min.

4) They would probably reach, From our gym, one
end to the other [3   A] long way.

<u>Strange but true</u>

1. 40 workbooks, 96 pgs, 10 Columns, 26 numbers/column, 98 pens. 5.888896 Numbers as in 12,13 or digits in numbers?

Each number after 9 has 2 digits or more in the numbers?

Numbers: 10 colums x 26 = 260 Multiple the number of numbers in each Column by how many Columns there are in one page. That would give you the number of numbers per page.

2nd method: I don't Know another one.

2. Numbers 1-9 already have 1 digit. So 5,888,896-1 = 5888887

Number of digits   Numbers
    2   100 (10-99)
    3   899 (100-999)
    4
    5
    6   11

(I confused myself with trying to solve individually for each digit. there's another way, but how). ?

3. $\frac{1 Second}{1 digit}$ = $\frac{5888896 \ seconds}{1}$ x $\frac{1 min}{60 \cdot sec}$ x $\frac{1 hr}{60 min}$ x $\frac{1 day}{24 hr}$

$\frac{68 \ day}{1}$ x $\frac{2 \ year}{730 \ day}$ = 0.50 year x $\frac{365 \ day}{1 \ year}$ = 183 or 184 digits per day.

4. Assume that the written numbers were all the same size How would you know how to calculate how long the digits stretch if you don't know how big a digit was? It's a big difference how long to judge it will strech if you don't know the length of an digit.

1) On each page he wrote 260 numbers. how I got it is there are 26 numbers on each column and there are 10 columns on each page

2) 1-9 (1 digit)
   10-99 (2
   100-999 (3
   1000-9999 (4
   10,000 99999 (5
   100,000 999999 (6
   1000.000 99,99,999 (7

   $\begin{array}{r} 9 \\ +99 \\ \hline 189 \\ 999 \\ \hline 1188 \end{array}$

   9999
   $\overline{12287}$
   99999
   $\overline{1 2 2 2 86}$
   999999
   $\overline{1.122.285}$

   $\begin{array}{r} 9 \\ 99 \\ \hline 189 \end{array}$ well I just have to write it all out

3) He would spend 5 hours and 20 mins.

4) The row reach 1 end of the gym to the other.

Strange but TRUE

1. ① (40 work books) (96 $\frac{pages}{WORK}$) (10 $\frac{columns}{Page}$) (26 $\frac{Spaces}{Columns}$) = 998,400 — not 1 million INCORRECT #'s

(10 columns) (26 $\frac{Spaces}{Columns}$) = $\boxed{260 \, Spaces}$

② 1 million ÷ 40 WB ÷ 96 = 260.4160

≈ $\boxed{260 \frac{Spaces}{Page}}$

2. 1,000,000

7(10) + 6(899,999) + 5(89999) + 4(8999) + 3(899) + 2(89) + 1(9)

take the # of Digits and multiply by the # of #'s with that many Digits and Add it all up. = $\boxed{5888876}$

3. 365 × 2 = 730 DAYS

5888896 seconds

$\frac{5888896}{730}$ = 8066.98 $\frac{Sec}{DAY}$ · $\frac{min}{60 Se}$ · $\frac{HR}{60 min}$ = 2.24 $\frac{HOUR}{DAY}$

4. $\frac{1 \, mill \, cm}{M}$ = 10000 meters

① She writes 1 million numbers in 40 workbooks each with 96 pages $\frac{1,000,000}{40 \times 96}$ = 260 numbers on each page.

②

numbers	number of digits	number of numbers
1 - 9	1	9
10 - 99	2	90
100 - 999	3	900
1,000 - 9,999	4	9,000
10,000 - 99,999	5	90,000
100,000ₛ - 999,999	6	900,000
1,000,000	7	1

The number of single digits is

$1 \times 9 + 2 \times 90 + 3 \times 900 + 4 \times 9,000 + 5 \times 90,000 + 6 \times 900,000 + 7 \times 1 = 5,888,896.$

③ $\frac{5,888,896 \text{ secs}}{2 \text{ years} \times 365 \text{ days}}$ = 8066.98 secs per day = 2.24 hours per day

④ Let each # = one box long
It there is 5,888,896 numbers then there is 5,888,896 boxes and assuming that a box is a square, the numbers would be 5,888,896 boxes long when laid end to end. So if one box had a side of 1 inch then the 1 of the column of numbers would be 5,888,896 inches of 490741,3 feet long or 163580.4 yards long.

Strange But True

a. $10 \times 26 = 260$ numbers

b. 1 Million / 40 books = $\frac{25000 \text{ numbers}}{1 \text{ book}}$ · $\frac{1 \text{ book}}{96 \text{ pages}}$ = $\frac{260 \quad 40}{96}$ numbers per page

2.		
9 1 digit numbers	$9 \cdot 1 = 9$	19
90 2 digit numbers	$90 \cdot 2 = 180$	180
900 3 digit numbers	$900 \cdot 3 = 2700$	2700
9000 4 digit numbers	$9000 \cdot 4 = 36000$	36000
90 000 5 digit numbers	$90000 \cdot 5 = 450000$	450000
900 000 6 digit numbers	$900000 \cdot 6 = 5400000$	5400000
1 7 digit number	$1 \cdot 7 = 7$	7
		5,888,896

3. $\frac{1 \text{ second}}{1 \text{ digit}}$ · 5888896 digits = $\frac{5888896 \text{ seconds}}{730 \text{ days}}$ = about 8067 seconds per day
or 134.45 minutes per day
or 2.24 hours per day
or 2 hours, 14 minutes, and 27 seconds per day
or 2 hours and 14.45 minutes per day

$\frac{365 \text{ days}}{1 \text{ year}}$ = $\frac{730 \text{ days}}{2 \text{ years}}$

By measuring different number sources I found numbers were generally written about $1/12$" wide.

$\frac{1}{12}$" · 5888896 digits = $490741\frac{1}{3}$"
= $40895' 1\frac{1}{3}$"
= 13661 yd 2ft $1\frac{1}{3}$ in
7 miles 1341 yds 2ft $1\frac{1}{3}$ in

Strange But True

1) You can multiply 26 numbers by 10 columns to get 260 numbers per page, or you can divide 1 million by (40 workbooks x 96 pages) to get 260.416, or there would be 260 numbers per page.

2) $1 \times 9 + 2 \times 90 + 3 \times 900 + 4 \times 9000 + 5 \times 90000 + 6 \times 900,000 + 7 \times 1 = 5,888,896.$ The above math is illustrating the specific number of digits (the first number in each pair of multiplied numbers) multiplied by the amount of numbers that have that many digits. Then, by adding them all up, we get the total number of digits written.

3) $5,888,896 \div (365 \times 2) = 8066.9,$ or ≈ 8067 seconds a day or 134.4 minutes 2.2 hours per day.

   I assume no leap year

4) If each digit were 5 millimeters wide, then it would stretch out $5 \times 5888896 = 29,444,480$ millimeters, or 29.4 kilometers.

2

Supermarket Carts

> **Develop an approach to a relatively unspecified task.**
>
> **Model a situation with a discrete linear function.**

Long Task

Task Description

This task asks students to analyze a situation in which supermarket carts are "nested" inside one another in a row. The students are given a scale diagram of nested carts.

The goal is to create a rule for the length of a row given the number of carts. Finally, the student is asked to give the rule for and the number of carts given a space s meters long.

Assumed Mathematical Background

Students need to have done work in algebra in which they have had a chance to work with simple linear functions and their applications. It is also essential that students have had some experience defining variables.

Core Elements of Performance

- formulate an approach to a task that is not fully specified
- model a structure symbolically—that is, recognize and generalize the pattern generated by a stack of nested supermarket carts
- become familiar with linear functions of a discrete variable n (that is, functions such as $y = 25n + 8$, where n is a whole number)
- set up and use such a function to model a given situation
- find the inverse of this function

Circumstances

Grouping:	Following a whole class introduction, students complete an individual written response.
Materials:	ruler and calculator (optional)
Estimated time:	45 minutes

Supermarket Carts

This problem gives you the chance to

- *think mathematically about supermarket carts*
- *create a rule that can be used to predict the length of storage space needed, given the number of carts*

The diagram on the right shows a drawing of a single supermarket cart.

The diagram below shows a drawing of 12 supermarket carts that have been "nested" together.

The drawings are $\frac{1}{24}$th the real size.

length

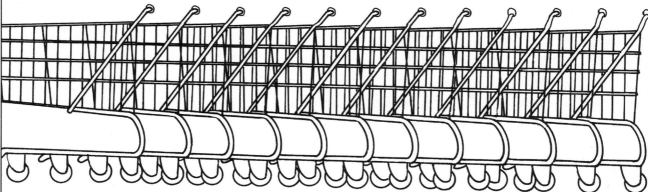

1. Create a rule that will tell you the length of storage space (*s*) needed when all you know is the number of supermarket carts to be stored. You will need to show *how* you built your rule; that is, explain which data you drew upon and tell how you used it.

2. Now show how you can figure out the number of carts that can fit in a space *s* meters long.

A Sample Solution

1. The length on the diagram is about 4 cm. Since the scale of the diagram is given as $\frac{1}{24}$, the length of a full-size supermarket cart is

   (4)(24) = 96 cm = 0.96 meters.

   When they are "nested," each scale-drawing supermarket cart sticks out behind the one in front of it by about 1.2 cm. (A good technique is to measure 10 carts in a row and divide by 10.) This is a full-size "sticking-out" length of about (1.2)(24) = 28.8 cm = 0.288 m.

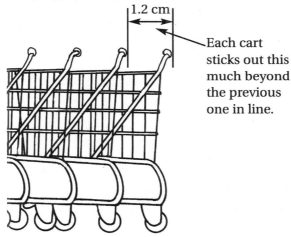

1.2 cm

Each cart sticks out this much beyond the previous one in line.

2. If the first cart measures 0.96 m and each other cart sticks out 0.288 m, then n carts take up $s = 0.96 + (0.288)(n - 1)$ meters.

   Rearranging for n gives $n = \frac{s - 0.96}{0.288} + 1$.

Task 2 · Using this Task

When you use this task, do not tell students that they should or may use a ruler. Use this task as an opportunity for students to decide what mathematical tools are needed.

Informal classroom use of this task is good when students are working on linear functions of the form $y = mx + b$. In this task, the independent variable is a whole number n that counts the number of carts. It may take some practice before students see the "meaning" of the two parameters in terms of the application. To illustrate, consider the formula for the space s in meters taken up by n carts:

$$s = 0.96 + (0.288)(n - 1)$$

This is a convenient form to use when computing s from n, but it is not in slope-intercept form. This form is

$$s = (0.288)(n) + 0.672$$

The slope m is $0.288 \frac{\text{meters}}{\text{cart}}$, which is the amount each cart sticks out beyond the previous cart in line. The y-intercept b is 0.672 meters, which is the part of the cart that doesn't stick out.

If you are using this task as part of a formal system of assessment, it should be presented to students with standardized instructions.

Extensions

Supermarket Carts can be extended for instructional purposes by having students do more work with this situation. They can graph the function for s in terms of n, and show how the graph can be used to find n from a given s or s for a given n. The results can be checked by actual measurements on the diagram for n up to 12.

Students can also be asked to come up with their own real-world examples illustrating linear functions.

For assessment purposes, other "stacking" or "nesting" situations can be given for students to analyze. A simple one is stacks of paper cups.

Characterizing Performance

This section offers a characterization of student responses and provides indications of the ways in which the students were successful or unsuccessful in engaging with and completing the task. The descriptions are keyed to the *Core Elements of Performance.* Our global descriptions of student work range from "The student needs significant instruction" to "The student's work meets the essential demands of the task." Samples of student work that exemplify these descriptions of performance are included below, accompanied by commentary on central aspects of each student's response. These sample responses are *representative;* they may not mirror the global description of performance in all respects, being weaker in some and stronger in others.

The characterization of student responses for this task is based on these *Core Elements of Performance:*
1. Formulate an approach to a task that is not fully specified.
2. Model a structure symbolically—that is, recognize and generalize the pattern generated by a stack of nested supermarket carts.
3. Become familiar with linear functions of a discrete variable n (that is, functions such as $y = 25n + 8$, where n is a whole number).
4. Set up and use such a function to model a given situation.
5. Find the inverse of this function.

Descriptions of Student Work

The student needs significant instruction

The task is engaged, but no rule or formula is devised.

Student A

The response does not show a workable strategy. Neither the scale drawing nor a constant proportion is used to formulate an approach to the task. The attention is concentrated on setting up and trying to solve a proportion.

The student needs some instruction.

The response provides a generalization, but does not provide any explanation of how the formula is constructed.

Task

2

There is a strong attempt to analyze the structure of the nested supermarket carts. This might be confined to a sound verbal description of the situation. The response may not use symbolic notation to represent the formula.

Student B

The response shows an attempt to analyze the structure of the nested carts. The scale drawing is used to figure out the length of one cart and the distance that a nested cart sticks out. Verbal description and chart combine to indicate how the structure grows, but no attempt has been made to create a formula or to generalize for a space *s* meters long. Notice that the response includes measurements to 3 decimal places.

The student's work needs to be revised.

There is convincing evidence that the student knows how the structure "grows." A general rule for *s* given *n* is devised. That rule may be cast in terms of the actual size of a cart; $s = 96 + 28.8(n-1)$. Alternatively, or in addition, the rule might be cast in terms of the length *l* of one cart: $s = l + \left(\frac{1}{3}\right)l(n-1)$. The response shows us how she/he knows that the formula is valid.

The response either does not succeed in providing or does not attempt to provide a formula for the length *s* in meters that is required for *n* carts.

Student C

The response is strong. The formula is $l + n - 1\left(\left(\frac{1}{3}\right)l\right) = s$, where *l* is the length of a cart. The student's articulation allows us to see how the student built the rule. The student does not reverse the formula correctly.

The student's work meets the essential demands of the task.

The student devises a general rule for *s* given *n*. That formula may be cast in terms of the actual size of a cart; $s = 96 + 28.8(n-1)$. Alternatively, or in addition, the formula might be cast in terms of *l*, the length of one cart: $s = l + \left(\frac{1}{3}\right)l(n-1)$. The student provides sufficient information to show how she/he constructed the formula and how she/he knows that her/his reasoning is valid. The student also demonstrates an ability to invert the formula to provide the length *s* in meters required for *n* carts.

Student D

All points are present and correct. The response is a pleasure to read. The level of articulation is remarkable. The student provides a full and comprehensive argument.

shopping Carts

① 1 shopping cart = 1l length

$$\frac{L}{S} = \frac{S}{L} = \frac{length}{shopping\ cut} = \frac{\text{length} (all\ shopping\ carts)}{length\ of\ shopping\ carts}$$

The length of one shopping cart will ~~help you~~ find proportion to All the shopping carts together.

② First you'll have to find the size of the first cart then you'd have to find how much of the cart sticks out when the two are put together. After this you can find how carts you need that will fit in the space that you want. If only given one length of the cart you can use proportion to find cart put together.

Length of the shopping cart in the drawing →

$\longleftrightarrow$
4 cm

4 cm ÷ 1/24 = 96 cm actual size of a cart

1.375 added for each basket at ¹/₆ᵗʰ size cm

16 ½ cm
―――――
12 carts

~~ᶻ ᴷ ᴴ ᴾ ᴹ ᴹ Ǝ ᴵ ᴵ ᴴ ᴹ ᴹ~~

# of extra carts	length of carts (cm)
0	4
1	5.375
2	6.75
3	8.125
4	9.5
	~~ᴵ ᴴ ᴵ ᴹ ᴹ ᴵ ᴴ ᴹ ᴵ ᴴ~~
5	10.876
6	12.25
7	13.625
8	15
9	~~Ⱥ~~ 16.375
10	17.75
11	
12	

Student C

1) $l + N + (\frac{1}{3}l) = 5$

$l + 11(\frac{1}{3}l) = 5$

example

$l = 14$

$N = 12$

$14 + [12 - 1(\frac{1}{3} \times 4)]$

$14 + 11(\frac{14}{3})$

$14 + \frac{154}{3}$

$14 + 51.3$

65.3 — space needed

Length of one cart (l) is to its one-third multiplied by number of carts minus 1. $\frac{1}{3}l$ will be the part of the cart which is not within the other cart. l will be the whole first cart and the 11 other carts will be $\frac{1}{3}$ of l.

2) $H + N - 1(\frac{1}{3} \times 14) = 89.3$

$14 - N - 1(\frac{14}{3}) = 65.3$

$(14 + \frac{11}{3}N) = 5$

$N - 1 = 65.3 - 14(\frac{14}{3}) \div \frac{14}{3}$

$= 51.3 - (\frac{14}{23}) \quad \frac{51.3}{4.66}$

$51.3(4.66) \quad 11.00$

$N - 1 = 11.00 \quad N = 12$

$N = 11 + 1$

$N - 1 = S - l \div \frac{1}{3}l$

Shopping Carts

Each shopping cart in the picture, when measured with a ruler is 1 7/16 inches long. Since the drawings are accurately scaled to 1/24 the real size, each cart is 345 inches long.

I also measured how much of a cart sticks out when two shopping carts are nested together. This length is 7/16 of an inch. To attain the accurate size, I multiplied 7/16 by 24 and got 10.5 inches. So the length of two carts nested together is 45 inches. Each additional cart would add an extra 10.5 inches.

Thus : (in inches)
$$S = 34.5 + 10.5 (n-1)$$
When S = length of storage space and
n = number of shopping carts to be stored
the 34.5 is the length of the first cart and 10.5 (n-1) is each additional length of a cart.

However, if I want to find the number n of shopping carts that will fit in a space S <u>meters</u> long, I should go through this same process using centimeters
So:

each shopping cart, based on the top drawing is 4cm long, or 96cm in the real size. Each additional cart is about

Student D

$$S = 96 + 28.8(n-1)$$

When you get this answer you would convert it to meters by dividing it by 100.

However, to make this problem even simpler, you can simply put the rule into meters.

thus: (in meters)

$$S = 0.96 + 0.288(n-1)$$

So we will test these rules by using the diagram. When measuring all the way across the 12 shopping carts, I get about 11.9 cm. So the real size is approximately 405.6 cm. ..o get meters divide by 100 = 4.056 m

By using the meter rule:

$$S = .96 + 0.288(n-1)$$
$$S = 0.96 + 0.288 (12-1)$$
$$S = 0.96 + 0.288(11)$$
$$S = 0.96 + 3.168$$
$$S = 4.128 \text{ meters}$$

The 2 answers I have gotten are fairly close, so I know that my rule is probably accurate. To find N by knowing S, let's convert the equation.

$$S = 0.96 + 0.288(n-1)$$
$$S - 0.96 = 0.288n - 0.288$$
$$S - 0.96 + 0.288 = 0.288 n$$
$$S - 0.672 = 0.288 n$$
$$\text{So} \rightarrow n = \frac{S - 0.672}{0.288}$$

3

Assessing Logo Design

Read and critique two real, yet contradictory, responses to a performance assessment.

Recognize and articulate common misconceptions concerning similarity.

Provide useful student commentary on how such misconceptions might be ameliorated.

Long Task

Task Description

This task asks students to read and critique two students' responses to a performance assessment "Tri-Tex Logo." In the original task, "Tri-Tex Logo," students were asked to determine the numbers of tiles of different colors that are required for an enlarged version of a simple logo. The student responses that are to be assessed here are real and are contradictory; thus, students are given the opportunity to confront and resolve conflict inherent in the misunderstanding that a given increase in linear dimension brings about a similar increase in area.

Assumed Mathematical Background

At minimum, students should have had some experience working problems involving perimeter, area, and proportional reasoning.

Core Elements of Performance

- recognize that an increase in linear dimensions of a shape does not imply a similar increase in area

- recognize a general rule that incorporates the notion that an increase in linear dimensions of a shape does not imply a similar increase in area

- follow and evaluate an argument that uses simple proportional reasoning

Circumstances

Grouping:	Students complete an individual written response.
Materials:	No special materials are needed for this task.
Estimated time:	45 minutes

Assessing Logo Design

This problem gives you the chance to

- *critique student misconceptions of mathematics*

In this task you are to imagine that you are a teacher assessing two students' responses to a math task. Below is the problem that the students were asked to solve. On the next pages the two students' solutions to the problem are given. You are asked to read the problem and two student responses. Then provide detailed feedback on each student's response to each part of the problem.

Logo Design
Here is the logo that has been proposed to Tri-Tex corporation:

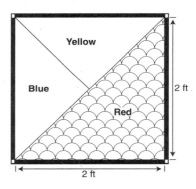

Tri-Tex Logo proposal:
The logo is 2 feet long and 2 feet wide.

It is made from tiny tiles of colored glass.

The red section uses 288 red tiles.

The blue section uses 144 blue tiles.

The yellow section uses 144 yellow tiles.

When the logo is mounted on the building, it will be framed by a black border.

This border will consist of a 1-tile-wide band of 40 long black tiles.

The director likes the proposal, but poses these questions. You must answer each of the director's questions.

1. How many tiles of each color will I need for a 4-ft × 4-ft logo? Show how you figured it out. (Do not forget the black border.)

2. Write a memo explaining how I can figure out the number of each color that I will need for any size of logo.

3. Suppose that there are only 6,000 red tiles. There are plenty of all the other colors. What is the size of the largest logo that can be made? Show how you figured it out.

1. How many tiles of each color will I need for a 4-ft × 4-ft logo? Show how you figured it out. (Do not forget about the black border.)

Student 1's answer	Student 2's answer

If the logo were 4ft. × 4ft you would need:
 	
 red - 288(2) = 576 tiles
 blue - 144(2) = 288 tiles
 yellow - 144(2) = 288 tiles
 black - 40(2) = 80 tiles
	$2^2 = 4$ 4×4 red = 288.4 =
	                    1152
	 $4^2 = 16 - 4$ blue = 144.4 = 576
	             yellow = 144.4 = 576
	             black = 40.4 = 160

Comment on Student 1's answer. What is correct? What is incorrect? How should the student revise the answer?	Comment on Student 2's answer. What is correct? What is incorrect? How should the student revise the answer?

2. Write a memo explaining how I can figure out the number of each color that I will need for any size of logo.

Student 1's answer	Student 2's answer
To find the number of each colored tile, you must Multiply the number of tiles by the amount of times the logo is enlarged. If the logo is changed from 2x2ft. to 6x6 ft. the logo has been enlarged 3 times the original size, so you must have 3 times the amount of tiles to build the logo.	First you find out how many tiles are in one square foot. 2 ft. x 2 ft. = 4 square feet $288 + 144 + 144 = \frac{576}{4} = 144$ 144 tiles in a square foot $\frac{144}{2} = 72$ red $\frac{144}{4} = 36$ blue, 36 yellow Then you multiply these numbers of tiles by the area of the square. For the black borders you would multiply the lengths of square by 20 feet.
Comment on Student 1's answer. What is correct? What is incorrect? How should the student revise the answer?	Comment on Student 2's answer. What is correct? What is incorrect? How should the student revise the answer?

3. Suppose that there are only 6,000 red tiles. There are plenty of all the other colors. What is the size of the largest logo that can be made? Show how you figured it out.

Student 1's answer	Student 2's answer
6000 ÷ 288 = 20.83 The largest logo that can be made by 6000 red tiles is 20x20 ft. because 6000 red tiles is a little over 20 times the amount of the original tiles needed to build a logo that was 2ft. x2ft.	The largest logo possible with 6000 red tiles is 9ft. x 9ft. 6000 ÷ 288 = 20.8 20.8 • 4 = 83.2 $\sqrt{832} \approx 9$ (9.1) 1. First I worked backwards in the process I came up with in #1 $9^2 = 81$ 81 ÷ 4 = 20.25 288 • 20.25 = 5832 red tiles 2. Then I did the process to make sure 9x9 would fit. $10^2 = 100$ 100 ÷ 4 = 25 288 • 25 = 7200 red tiles 3. Then I tried the next number up and it was over 6000 red tiles, so the answer must be 9x9.
Comment on Student 1's answer. What is correct? What is incorrect? How should the student revise the answer?	Comment on Student 2's answer. What is correct? What is incorrect? How should the student revise the answer?

Task **3**

A Sample Solution

1. How many tiles of each color will I need for a 4-ft × 4-ft logo? Show how you figured it out. (Do not forget about the black border.)

Student 1's answer	Student 2's answer

If the logo were 4ft.×4ft you would need:
 	
red – 288(2)= 576 tiles
blue – 144(2)= 288 tiles
yellow – 144(2)= 288 tiles
black – 40(2) = 80 tiles
	$2^2 = 4$ 4×4 red = 288·4=
	                                1152
	$4^2 = 16-4$ blue = 144·4= 576
	               yellow = 144·4 =576
	               black =40·4 = 160

Comment on Student 1's answer. What is correct? What is incorrect? How should the student revise the answer?	Comment on Student 2's answer. What is correct? What is incorrect? How should the student revise the answer?
Here the student assumes that the number of tiles necessary for a 4-by-4 logo is double the number of each color that is required for a 2-by-2 design. The student does not explain how she/he knows that this is true but this work shows the calculations clearly. The calculations for the number of black tiles is the only one that is correct. The numbers given for red, blue, and yellow tiles is incorrect. The student should revise his/her work by looking at what happens to the area of a square when its length of side is doubled.	In this task the student has calculated that the number of each color of tiles should be 4 times that required for the 2-by-2-design. The student has noticed that the area of the 4-by-4 logo is not just double the area of the 2-by-2 logo. The new area is 4 times that of the area of the 2-by-2 logo. Thus the student calculates correctly that the number of red, blue, and yellow tiles will be 4 times greater than the original design. The student also calculates that the number of black tiles will be 4 times greater. The black tiles on each model form a single black band. Therefore for a 4-by-4 logo the number of black tiles is simply double that required in a 2-by-2 logo.

2. Write a memo explaining how I can figure out the number of each color that I will need for any size of logo.

Student 1's answer	Student 2's answer
To find the number of each colored tile, you must multiply the number of tiles by the amount of times the logo is enlarged. If the logo is changed from 2x2 ft. to 6x6 ft. the logo has been enlarged 3 times the original size, so you must have 3 times the amount of tiles to build the logo.	First you find out how many tiles are in one square foot. 2 ft. × 2 ft. = 4 square feet 288 + 144 + 144 = $\frac{576}{4}$ =144 144 tiles in a square foot $\frac{144}{2}$ = 72 red $\frac{144}{4}$ = 36 blue, 36 yellow Then you multiply these numbers of tiles by the area of the square. For the black borders you would multiply the lengths of square by 20 feet.
Comment on Student 1's answer. What is correct? What is incorrect? How should the student revise the answer?	Comment on Student 2's answer. What is correct? What is incorrect? How should the student revise the answer?

The student explains that the number of tiles needed for any size of logo is found by multiplying "by the amount of times the logo is enlarged." The student does not realize that the ratio of the area of the enlarged figure and the original is equal to the square of the ratios of the linear dimensions.

The student describes how to figure out the number of tiles in any size of logo. First, the student notices that it is useful to figure out the area of one square foot. She/he does this by finding the total number of tiles in a 2-by-2 logo. This is the number needed for a 4-square-foot logo. From this the number of each color in a 1-by-1 logo is calculated. The student then concludes without using symbolic notation that the number of each color can be found by $72n + 36n + 36n$.

The student makes a slight error in describing how to find the number of black tiles. The student says to multiply by "20 feet" rather than multiply by "20 tiles."

Task

3. Suppose that there are only 6,000 red tiles. There are plenty of all the other colors. What is the size of the largest logo that can be made? Show how you figured it out.

Student 1's answer	Student 2's answer
6000 ÷ 288 = 20.83 The largest logo that can be made by 6000 red tiles is 20x20 ft. because 6000 red tiles is a little over 20 times the amount of the original tiles needed to build a logo that was 2ft. x 2ft.	The Largest logo possible with 6000 red tiles is 9ft. x 9ft. 6000 ÷ 288 = 20.8 20.8 • 4 = 83.2 $\sqrt{832} \approx 9$ 1. First I worked backwards in the process I came up with in #1 9² = 81 81 ÷ 4 = 20.25 288 • 20.25 = 5832 red tiles 2. Then I did the process to make sure 9 x 9 would fit. 10² = 100 100 ÷ 4 = 25 288 • 25 = 7200 red tiles 3. Then I tried the next number up and it was over 6000 red tiles, so the answer must be 9 x 9.
Comment on Student 1's answer. What is correct? What is incorrect? How should the student revise the answer?	Comment on Student 2's answer. What is correct? What is incorrect? How should the student revise the answer?
The student's answer and procedure is incorrect; 6,000 ÷ 288 gives the number of 2-by-2 logos that could be made.	The student answers this part correctly, but it is quite difficult to follow the explanation. For example, the student divides 6,000 by 288 and multiplies by 4. We do not know why the student does this. Given the student's answer to part 2, we would expect 6,000 ÷ 72 to be an understandable procedure.

Using this Task

Give the students the task and ask them to work individually. Remind students that it is their task to figure out what each student is saying and to assess the correctness of the response.

Extensions

The role reversal activity in which the students act as teacher is an excellent way to assess or probe students' conceptual understanding. This activity can be carried out using student work generated in the classroom.

An interesting activity that would provide closure for students would be to make an overhead of the task and have a group discussion of the correctness of student responses. This would be particularly valuable to students who judged Student 1's response better than Student 2's.

A specific extension would be to ask students to plan a piece of teaching material that they consider to be useful to the students who were unable to provide an acceptable response to the task.

Task **Characterizing Performance**

This section offers a characterization of student responses and provides indications of the ways in which the students were successful or unsuccessful in engaging with and completing the task. The descriptions are keyed to the *Core Elements of Performance*. Our global descriptions of student work range from "The student needs significant instruction" to "The student's work meets the essential demands of the task." Samples of student work that exemplify these descriptions of performance are included below, accompanied by commentary on central aspects of each student's response. These sample responses are *representative;* they may not mirror the global description of performance in all respects, being weaker in some and stronger in others.

The characterization of student responses for this task is based on these *Core Elements of Performance:*

1. Recognize that an increase in linear dimensions of a shape does not imply a similar increase in area.
2. Recognize a general rule that incorporates the notion that an increase in linear dimensions of a shape does not imply a similar increase in area.
3. Follow and evaluate an argument that uses simple proportional reasoning.

Descriptions of Student Work

The student needs significant instruction.

The student understands that their task is to assess other students' work. Typically, the student assumes without question the correctness of Student 1's response and the incorrectness of Student 2's response. In addition, the response may be impressed with the clarity in Student 1's response and the apparent confusion of Student 2's response.

Student A

The student recognizes that a ratio ought to be set up, but assumes incorrectly that ratio is simply the ratio of the sides. As a consequence, this response evaluates everything in Student 1's response as correct and everything in Student 2's response as incorrect.

The student needs some instruction.

This response recognizes that the ratio of the areas of similar figures is the square of the ratios of the linear dimensions. The student has difficulty articulating the general rule and may be unable to determine the largest size of logo that can be made with 6,000 red tiles.

Student B

The student uses a geometric argument to critique the students' responses. In questions 1 and 2, her analysis of the responses is correct. She is accurate in her account of how border tiles and area tiles ought to be computed. In response to question 3, however, her critique is superficial and incorrect. She defines everything in Student 1's response as correct and everything in Student 2's response as incorrect.

The student's work needs to be revised.

The student shows understanding that the ratio of the areas of similar figures is the square of the ratios of the linear dimensions. The response notes the incorrectness of Student 1's response and is not seduced by its apparent clarity. In addition it is not intimidated by either the sophistication or the confusion in Student 2's response. The student may be shaky in the generalization required in question 2 or may be unable to figure out the largest size logo that can be made with 6,000 red tiles.

Student C

The student resolves the conflict provided in questions 1 and 3. In question 1, she presents a simple proportional reasoning argument that works, although she does not catch the distinction between the black perimeter tiles and the other area tiles. In question 3, she computes correctly the largest logo that can be made using 6,000 red tiles. She notices the confusion in the method set by Student 2, but finesses this by saying that it represents a trial-and-error approach and her own method is more direct.

In question 2 the student does not recognize that Student 2 is attempting to articulate a generalization for computing the number of colors that are required for any size of tile. The critique of Student 2 falls into an analysis of a specific case.

The student's work meets the essential demands of the task.

The student uses an algebraic or geometric argument to outline the general correctness of Student 2's response. The student either notes that you must consider what happens to the area or sets up a simple proportional

Task

reasoning argument to illustrate the misconceptions in Student 1's response and the correctness of that of Student 2.

Student D

This student shows evidence of being able to differentiate between the effect of enlargement on the perimeter and area of the logo. The student identifies correctly the aspects that are correct in each part of the students' responses. In response to question 1 and question 2, the student notes that attention must be paid to the concomitant changes in area that the increases in perimeter bring about. The student's critique of both responses demonstrates a highly consolidated understanding of this relationship. This student recognizes the confusion in Student 2's response to question 3. The student's own clarity and understanding, however, is illustrated in the articulate critique of Student 1's incorrect response to question 3.

Student A

1. How many tiles of each color will I need for a 4-ft × 4-ft logo? Show how you figured it out. (Do not forget about the black border.)

Student 1's answer	Student 2's answer

If the logo were 4ft.×4ft you would need:
 	
red -288(2)= 576 tiles
blue- 144(2)= 288 tiles
yellow - 144(2)= 288 tiles
black- 40(2) = 80 tiles
	$2^2 = 4$ 4×4 red = 288·4=
	                              1152
	$4^2 = 16-4$ blue = 144·4= 576
	                  yellow = 144·4 =576
	                  black =40·4 = 160

Comment on Student 1's answer. What is correct? What is incorrect? How should the student revise the answer?	Comment on Student 2's answer. What is correct? What is incorrect? How should the student revise the answer?
Everything is correct. He has all answers the same as ½ which is the ratio of sides.	Nothing is correct. Student B squared 2 and multiplied everything by 4. He should have used the equation ½=x/y

Student A

2. Write a memo explaining how I can figure out the number of each color that I will need for any size of logo.

Student 1's answer	Student 2's answer
To find the number of each colored tile, you must Multiply the number of tiles by the amount of times the logo is enlarged. If the logo is changed from 2×2ft. to 6×6ft. the logo has been enlarged 3times the original size, so you must have 3 times the amount of tiles to build the logo.	First you find out how many tiles are in one square foot. 2 ft. × 2 ft. = 4 square feet 288 + 144 + 144 = $\frac{576}{4}$ = 144 144 tiles in a square foot $\frac{144}{2}$ = 72 red $\frac{144}{4}$ = 36 blue, 36 yellow Then you multiply these numbers of tiles by the area of the square. For the black borders you would multiply the lengths of square by 20 feet.
Comment on Student 1's answer. What is correct? What is incorrect? How should the student revise the answer?	Comment on Student 2's answer. What is correct? What is incorrect? How should the student revise the answer?
It's somewhat right, but what if it's enlarged to 7 by 7 ft? You need to Know the side ratio, which is 2/x. Than you get the equation 2/x = Tiles sm/tiles lrg	This is a very lengthy and wrong answer, all you need to know is the side ratio to get the equation 2/x = Tiles sm/lg

Student A

3. Suppose that there are only 6,000 red tiles. There are plenty of all the other colors. What is the size of the largest logo that can be made? Show how you figured it out.

Student 1's answer	Student 2's answer
6000 ÷ 288 = 20.83 The largest logo that can be made by 6000 red tiles is 20 x 20 ft. because 6000 red tiles is a little over 20 times the amount of the original tiles needed to build a logo that was 2ft. x 2ft.	The largest logo possible with 6000 red tiles is 9ft. x 9ft. 6000 ÷ 288 = 20.8 20.8 • 4 = 83.2 $\sqrt{832} \approx 9$ 1. First I worked backwards in the process I came up with in #1 $9^2 = 81$ $81 \div 4 = 20.25$ $288 \cdot 20.25 = 5832$ red tiles 2. Then I did the process to make sure 9 x 9 would fit. $10^2 = 100$ $100 \div 4 = 25$ $288 \cdot 25 = 7200$ red tiles 3. Then I tried the next number up and it was over 6000 red tiles, so the answer must be 9 x 9.
Comment on Student 1's answer. What is correct? What is incorrect? How should the student revise the answer?	Comment on Student 2's answer. What is correct? What is incorrect? How should the student revise the answer?
This is a good way to figure this problem out. good job!	This is very wrong. If you know that there is 288 tiles in a 2x2 sign. Than you can divide 6000 by 288 to find the side measure.

1. How many tiles of each color will I need for a 4-ft × 4-ft logo? Show how you figured it out. (Do not forget about the black border.)

Student 1's answer	Student 2's answer

If the logo were 4ft.x4ft you would need:

red - 288(2) = 576 tiles
blue - 144(2) = 288 tiles
yellow - 144(2) = 288 tiles
black - 40(2) = 80 tiles

$2^2 = 4$

$4^2 = 16 - 4$

4x4 red = 288.4 = 1152
blue = 144.4 = 576
yellow = 144.4 = 576
black = 40.4 = 160

Comment on Student 1's answer. What is correct? What is incorrect? How should the student revise the answer?	Comment on Student 2's answer. What is correct? What is incorrect? How should the student revise the answer?

The number of tiles for the black is correct because in that one you are finding the perimeter so - you would double the length of each side and then multiply it by the number of sides, so it would be 20·4=80. The the numbers of tiles for Red, Yellow, and blue are wrong because they multiplied them by two, The perimeter is twice is big but the area is four times as big so the numbers should be multiplied by four.

The answers for Red yellow and blue are correct, the answer for the black tiles is incorrect because for perimeter it is only twice as long not 4 times as long as it is four area, so that 40 would by multiplied by 2 instead of 4

Student B

2. Write a memo explaining how I can figure out the number of each color that I will need for any size of logo.

Student 1's answer	Student 2's answer
To find the number of each colored tile, you must multiply the number of tiles by the amount of times the logo is enlarged. If the logo is changed from 2x2ft. to 6x6ft. the logo has been enlarged 3 times the original size, so you must have 3 times the amount of tiles to build the logo.	First you find out how many tiles are in one square foot. 2 ft. x 2 ft. = 4 square feet 288 + 144 + 144 = $\frac{576}{4}$ = 144 144 tiles in a square foot $\frac{144}{2}$ = 72 red $\frac{144}{4}$ = 36 blue, 36 yellow Then you multiply these numbers of tiles by the area of the square. For the black borders you would multiply the lengths of square by 20 feet.
Comment on Student 1's answer. What is correct? What is incorrect? How should the student revise the answer?	Comment on Student 2's answer. What is correct? What is incorrect? How should the student revise the answer?
It would be 3 times the Original size but that is not the way you would figure it out. You would find the area of the small square 2.2=4 then you would find the area of the large square 6.6 = 36. You would divide the area of the large square by the area of the small square 304 ⇒ 9 then you would take the number of tiles in the small square 288.9=2592 144.9=1296 FOR perimeter you would times 10 by the length 6: 6.10 =60 and multiply that number by 2 2.60=120	They get the numbers FOR the COLORed tiles right. FOR the black borders you would multiply the length OF the square by 10. 8.10=80 and then multiply that number by 2. 2.80 = 160

3. Suppose that there are only 6,000 red tiles. There are plenty of all the other colors. What is the size of the largest logo that can be made? Show how you figured it out.

Student 1's answer	Student 2's answer
6000 ÷ 288 = 20.83 The largest logo that can be made by 6000 red tiles is 20x20 ft. because 6000 red tiles is a little over 20 times the amount of the original tiles needed to build a logo that was 2ft. x2ft.	The largest logo possible with 6000 red tiles is 9ft. x 9ft. 6000 ÷ 288 = 20.8 20.8 • 4 = 83.2 $\sqrt{832} \approx 9$ 1. First I worked backwards in the process I came up with a #1 $9^2 = 81$ 81 ÷ 4 = 20.25 288 • 20.25 = 5832 red tiles 2. Then I did the process to make sure 9 x 9 would fit. $10^2 = 100$ 100 ÷ 4 = 25 288 • 25 = 7200 red tiles 3. Then I tried the next number up and it was over 6000 red tiles, so the answer must be 9 x 9.
Comment on Student 1's answer. What is correct? What is incorrect? How should the student revise the answer?	Comment on Student 2's answer. What is correct? What is incorrect? How should the student revise the answer?
Student A did everything correctly just as I would have done.	Student B is incorrect

1. How many tiles of each color will I need for a 4-ft × 4-ft logo? Show how you figured it out. (Do not forget about the black border.)

Student 1's answer	Student 2's answer
If the logo were 4ft.×4ft you would need: red - 288(2)= 576 tiles blue - 144(2)= 288 tiles yellow - 144(2)= 288 tiles black - 40(2) = 80 tiles	$2^2 = 4$ 4×4 red = 288.4= 1152 $4^2 = 16-4$ blue = 144.4= 576 yellow = 144.4 =576 black = 40.4 = 160

Comment on Student 1's answer. What is correct? What is incorrect? How should the student revise the answer?	Comment on Student 2's answer. What is correct? What is incorrect? How should the student revise the answer?
You cannot just multiply the number of tiles by 2 just because 4 is twice the number of the original logo's sides. It should have been multiplied to their ratio of proportion which is 4. $\frac{2^2}{2^2} : \frac{4^2}{4^2} = 4:16 \frac{16}{4} \Rightarrow 4$ Each no. of tiles of each color must be multiplied to 4 to find no of tiles of each color for 4×4 logo.	The first process were okay but this process couldn't be understand why $4^2 = 16-4$ and subtract the (no. of tiles) 4 from square of 4. This were not necessary. Simply multiply area or square of original logo with the no. of tiles of each color. Well, in this case, that area of the 2×2 logo is equal to proportion of area of 2×2 and 4×4. This is 4:16 = 4 or ¼. For every case, take their ratio of proportion and multiply by number of tiles. Remember to put the logo to the numerator.

2. Write a memo explaining how I can figure out the number of each color that I will need for any size of logo.

Student 1's answer	Student 2's answer
To find the number of each colored tile, you must Multiply the number of tiles by the amount of times the logo is enlarged. If the logo is changed from 2x2ft. to 6x6ft. the logo has been enlarged 3 times the original size, so you must have 3 times the amount of tiles to build the logo.	First you find out how many tiles are in one square foot. 2 ft. x 2 ft. = 4 square feet $288 + 144 + 144 = \frac{576}{4} = 144$ 144 tiles in a square foot $\frac{144}{2} = 72$ red $\frac{144}{4} = 36$ blue, 36 yellow Then you multiply these numbers of tiles by the area of the square. For the black borders you would multiply the lengths of square by 20 feet.
Comment on Student 1's answer. What is correct? What is incorrect? How should the student revise the answer?	Comment on Student 2's answer. What is correct? What is incorrect? How should the student revise the answer?

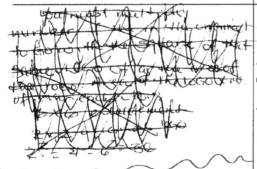

Wrong. You must multiply no. of tiles for each color by the ratio of proportion of the area of the two figure, the original and the enlargement.

A =
$2^2 : 6^2$
$4 : 36$ $\frac{36}{4} = \frac{9}{1} \rightarrow$ 9 should be multiplied to each no. of tiles of each color

(~~this is~~)
The first steps were okay. We find that 144 is no. of tiles per square foot. The next solution should be $\frac{1}{2}(4^2) = \frac{16}{2} = 8$. Since no. of tiles is half the square, multiply 144 by 8 red tiles = 1152 red (~~tiles~~) tiles The number of blue and yellow tiles is half that of red $\frac{1}{4}$ of the square, $\frac{16}{4} = 4$, multiply 144 by 4, 576 Blue and yellow tiles
These written under not necessary were only ~~applicable~~ for 1x1 logo, since 144 is the number of tiles. 4^2 is area of the enlargement.

Student C

3. Suppose that there are only 6,000 red tiles. There are plenty of all the other colors.
What is the size of the largest logo that can be made? Show how you figured it out.

Student 1's answer	Student 2's answer
$6000 \div 288 = 20.83$ The largest logo that can be made by 6000 red tiles is 20x20 ft. because 6000 red tiles is a little over 20 times the amount of the original tiles needed to build a logo that was 2ft. x2ft. $\frac{288}{2} = \frac{6000}{x}$ → $\frac{288x}{288} = \frac{6000(2)}{288}$ → 41.66 ♦ you can also use this other than $\frac{6000}{144}$ then continue the process.	The largest logo possible with 6000 red tiles is 9ft. x 9ft. $6000 \div 288 = 20.8$ $20.8 \cdot 4 = 83.2$ $\sqrt{832} \approx 9$ (9.1) 1. First I worked backwards in the process I came up with a #1 $9^2 = 81$ $81 \div 4 = 20.25$ $288 \cdot 20.25 = 5832$ red tile 2. Then I did the process to make sure 9×9 would fit. $10^2 = 100$ $100 \div 4 = 25$ $288 \cdot 25 = 7200$ red tiles 3. Then I tried the next number up and it was over 6000 red tiles, so the answer must be 9×9.
Comment on Student 1's answer. What is correct? What is incorrect? How should the student revise the answer?	Comment on Student 2's answer. What is correct? What is incorrect? How should the student revise the answer?
Everything is wrong. The previous problem mentioned of 144 is no. of tiles in a sq. ft. Instead of dividing the number of tiles from the original logo to 6000, 144 should have been divided to 6000. To get 144, you add the number of tiles in the 2x2 logo and divide it by the ratio of its area with that of 4x4 in terms of proportion. The quotient will be half of the square footage of the entire logo. Multiply to 2 to get the other half, too. The product would be the area of the square logo, get the square root to find the length of each side.	$\frac{6,000}{144}$ tiles in a square foot 41.66—half of the square feet of the logo $(41.6)2 = 83.3$ square feet of the logo ★ To find the length of each side find square root of square footage $\sqrt{83.3} = 9.13$ units or 9units size of largest logo that can be made: 9×9 Student B used a trial by error by testing the side length of a particular square. The above method is a direct one.

Student D

1. How many tiles of each color will I need for a 4-ft × 4-ft logo? Show how you figured it out. (Do not forget about the black border.)

Student 1's answer	Student 2's answer
If the logo were 4ft. x 4ft you would need: red - 288(2) = 576 tiles blue - 144(2) = 288 tiles yellow - 144(2) = 288 tiles black - 40(2) = 80 tiles	$2^2 = 4$ $4^2 = 16 - 4$ 4x4 red = 288.4 = 1152 blue = 144.4 = 576 yellow = 144.4 = 576 black = 40.4 = 160
Comment on Student 1's answer. What is correct? What is incorrect? How should the student revise the answer?	**Comment on Student 2's answer.** What is correct? What is incorrect? How should the student revise the answer?
The proportion between the 2x2 logo and the 4x4 logo is not 1 to 2. The area of the 2x2 logo = 4 and the area of the 4x4 logo = 16, Therefore being 1 to 4. You have the right idea, just not the correct proportions. Instead of multiplying the tiles by 2, you would need to multiply them by 4. The tiles are going to fill up the <u>area</u> of the logo. You would need to calculate the areas. You calculated the border tiles correctly. Since you need to find the area, the proportion is 1 to 2. Very good!	For the most part, pretty good - You got the idea that you must calculate the area to get the red, blue, + yellow tiles. But the black tiles are for the border. The area for the border is not being multiplied by 4. Think of the borders as an outline. You need 40 tile for a 2 x 2 logo. You want to double each side of the logo, therefore you need to double the number of tiles. 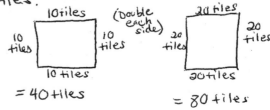 = 40 tiles = 80 tiles

2. Write a memo explaining how I can figure out the number of each color that I will need for any size of logo.

Student 1's answer	Student 2's answer
To find the number of each colored tile, you must multiply the number of tiles by the amount of times the logo is enlarged. If the logo is changed from 2x2ft. to 6x6 ft. the logo has been enlarged 3 times the original size, so you must have 3 times the amount of tiles to build the logo.	First you find out how many tiles are in one square foot. 2 ft. x 2 ft. = 4 square feet 288 + 144 + 144 = $\frac{576}{4}$ = 144 144 tiles in a square foot $\frac{144}{2}$ = 72 red $\frac{144}{4}$ = 36 blue, 36 yellow Then you multiply these numbers of tiles by the area of the square. For the black borders you would multiply the lengths of square by 20 feet.
Comment on Student 1's answer. What is correct? What is incorrect? How should the student revise the answer?	Comment on Student 2's answer. What is correct? What is incorrect? How should the student revise the answer?
Correct only for borders, the rest of the tiles, you must multiply the # of tiles by the amount of times the area of the logo is enlarged. The tiles are being filled inside the logo not just around it. If the logo is changed from 2x2ft to 6x6 ft. The area has been enlarged 9 times ($\frac{36}{4}$). Therefore you need 9 times the amount of tiles to fill the inside of the logo. For the border, since it is only around the logo, you need only to multiply the number of tiles by the amount of times the logo is enlarged. Which is what you got correct	For the most part, correct your process and answer for the red, yellow, and blue tiles is correct. For the border, however, 40 tiles for 2x2 ft logo are needed. This means that 10 tiles are needed for each 2 ft. Therefore, there are 10 tiles needed for every 2 ft. which reduces to 5 tiles every ft. Then to find the number of black tiles, you need to multiply the number of feet on the side of the logo by 5 then multiply that by 4 sides.

3. Suppose that there are only 6,000 red tiles. There are plenty of all the other colors. What is the size of the largest logo that can be made? Show how you figured it out.

Student 1's answer	Student 2's answer
6000 ÷ 288 = 20.83 The largest logo that can be made by 6000 red tiles is 20×20 ft. because 6000 red tiles is a little over 20 times the amount of the original tiles needed to build a logo that was 2ft. ×2ft.	The largest logo possible with 6000 red tiles is 9ft. × 9ft. 6000 ÷ 288 = 20.8 20.8 · 4 = 83.2 $\sqrt{832} \approx 9$ (9.1 above) 1. First I worked backward in the process I came up with a #1 $9^2 = 81$ 81 ÷ 4 = 20.25 288 · 20.25 = 5832 red tile 2. Then I did the process to make sure 9×9 would fit. $10^2 = 100$ 100 ÷ 4 = 25 288 · 25 = 7200 red tiles 3. Then I tried the next number up and it was over 6000 red tiles, so the answer must be 9×9.
Comment on Student 1's answer. What is correct? What is incorrect? How should the student revise the answer?	Comment on Student 2's answer. What is correct? What is incorrect? How should the student revise the answer?
Incorrect. Again, you need to look at the red part. At 2×2ft., 288 red tiles were needed which means that 288 tiles filled up the space of 2ft.² You know that the area of the red tiles is ½ of the whole logo. To better understand it you can set up a proportional ratio: $\frac{288 \text{ tiles}}{2 \text{ ft}} = \frac{6000 \text{ ti}}{x}$ Cross multiply X = 41.67 = area of red area of triangle = $\frac{bh}{2}$ $A = \frac{83.33}{2}$ $\sqrt{83.33} = 9.13$. The dimensions would be about 9×9 ft.	YES. I'm a little confused on why you had to do #'s 2 and 3. They are unnecessary.

6:10

<u>35 min. total</u>

1. 2×2   Red = 288
         blue = 144
         Yellow = 144
         border = 40

4×4

10 tiles Every 2 ft
5 tiles every ft.

16 ft × 5 = 80 border tiles

#of Tiles → $\frac{288}{2}$ = 1152 Red tiles / 8

$\frac{144}{1}$ = area → 576 blue tiles / 4   576 Yellow tiles

80
1152
576
+ 576
2384 Tiles

2. by cross Multiplication or proportionality
For Red tiles $\frac{288}{2}$ = $\frac{\#of tiles}{(area)}$ For blue tiles + yellow tiles $\frac{144}{1}$
For border There are 5 tiles to Every ft.

3. $\frac{288}{2}$ = $\frac{6,000}{41.67}$ = area of red A= $\frac{bh}{2}$ A= $\frac{83.33}{2}$

$\sqrt{83.33}$ = 9.13 The Dimensions would be about 9×9 ft

15 min.

Designing a Staircase

Use the concept of slope in an applied context involving staircases.

Operate with an inequality that limits the overall size of an allowable stair step.

Figure out a choice of rise and run that meets given requirements on stair size and slope.

Long Task

Task Description

The task presents guidelines on step size and steepness allowable in staircases. The students are then asked to design a staircase that joins one floor with another floor 11 feet above it. The main job is to determine how many steps are required, and what size they must be.

Assumed Mathematical Background

Students should have done some work with the concept of slope of a line thought of as the (vertical) rise divided by the (horizontal) run of any section of the line.

Core Elements of Performance

- use the concept of slope (rise over run) in the setting of a staircase of repeated equal steps

- work with inequalities that specify the minimum and maximum allowable slope

- work with inequalities that specify minimum and maximum step size (where step size is measured as twice the rise plus the run)

- find the dimensions of a step that is within the guidelines and that can be used to span a given vertical distance

Circumstances

Grouping:	Students complete an individual written response.
Materials:	ruler and calculator
Estimated time:	45 minutes

Designing a Staircase

55

Designing a Staircase

This problem gives you the chance to

- *design a staircase that meets certain guidelines*
- *use the concept of slope in a practical situation*

Design a staircase that has a total rise of 11 feet and that meets the design guidelines given below.

Communicate your design decisions clearly: how many risers and treads are there, and what size are they?

Include your calculations.

Show how each design guideline is met.

Design Guidelines
- The slope of the staircase must be between 0.55 and 0.85.

- Twice the rise plus the run must be between 24 and 25 inches.

- There can be no irregular steps: Each step must be the same size.

Some useful terms

tread: the horizontal part of a step

run: the length of the tread

riser: the vertical part of a step

rise: the height of the riser

slope: a measure of the steepness of a staircase found by dividing the riser height (rise) by the tread length (run):

$$\text{slope} = \frac{\text{rise}}{\text{run}}$$

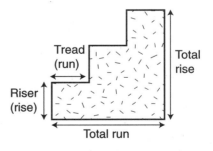

A Sample Solution

There are many approaches to this problem. One is to guess a number of steps, say 20 steps. Since the stairs must rise 11 feet = 132 inches, each riser is 132 ÷ 20 = 6.6 inches in height. It is required that twice the riser (13.2 inches) plus the tread must be between 24 and 25 inches. Let's choose 24.5 inches. This makes the tread 11.3 inches. What slope is this? It is 6.6 ÷ 11.3 ≈ 0.58. This is within the required limits 0.55 ≤ slope ≤ 0.85. So this design works.

Summary: There are 20 steps, each with the dimensions riser = 6.6 inches and tread = 11.3 inches. The slope is about 0.58.

Another Sample Solution

Here is a more systematic solution with more of the reasoning supplied:

Use the notation m = slope, R = riser height (in inches), and T = tread length (in inches).

Since slope = $m = \dfrac{\text{rise}}{\text{run}} = \dfrac{\text{riser height}}{\text{tread length}} = \dfrac{R}{T}$, the relation $R = mT$ always holds.

Choose an arbitrary slope m for the staircase within the given range, say $m = 0.75$. Then $R = 0.75T$.

The requirement "twice the rise plus the run must be between 24 and 25 inches" can be expressed as: 24 inches $\leq 2R + T \leq$ 25 inches. Substituting for R and solving for T, we get:

$24 \leq 2(0.75T) + T \leq 25$
$24 \leq 1.5T + T \leq 25$
$24 \leq 2.5T \leq 25$
$9.6 \leq T \leq 10$

Since $R = 0.75T$, 7.2 inches $\leq R \leq$ 7.5 inches.

The steps altogether must rise 11 feet (or 132 inches), and the individual steps must all be the same size. This means 132 ÷ R = a whole number. Checking the values of R at the two extremes:

132 inches ÷ 7.2 inches = 18.3 steps and 132 inches ÷ 7.5 inches = 17.6 steps.

Task 4

That means our staircase must have 18 steps. Since all the steps must be the same height, $R = 132 \div 18 = 7\frac{1}{3}$ inches, and $T = \frac{R}{0.75} = 9\frac{7}{9}$ inches.

Summary: There are 18 steps, each with the dimensions $R = 7\frac{1}{3}$ inches, and $T = 9\frac{7}{9}$ inches. The slope is 0.75.

We can double-check that our staircase meets the guideline 24 inches $\leq 2R + T \leq 25$ inches: $2\left(7\frac{1}{3}\right) + 9\frac{7}{9} = 24\frac{4}{9}$ inches.

Since 24 inches $\leq 24\frac{4}{9}$ inches ≤ 25 inches, the staircase is within the guidelines.

Still Another Sample Solution

A more thorough treatment comes through starting with a number N of steps, finding the required riser height $R = 132 \div N$, finding the maximum and minimum tread length T for this value of R using the requirement 24 inches $\leq 2R + T \leq 25$ inches, and computing the slope for each of these two tread lengths. This can be done for all the values of N that lead to acceptable slopes, and the result can be put in a table.

The key is in the computed slope. Those slopes that fall within the limits of 0.55 and 0.85 are entered in bold. These represent possible staircases. (Values are rounded off.)

N	$R = \dfrac{132}{N}$	$T = 24 - 2R$	slope $= \dfrac{R}{T}$	$T = 25 - 2R$	slope $= \dfrac{R}{T}$
16	8.25	7.5	1.1	8.5	0.97
17	7.76	8.48	0.92	9.48	**0.82**
18	7.33	9.34	**0.78**	10.34	**0.71**
19	6.95	10.1	**0.69**	11.1	**0.63**
20	6.6	10.8	**0.61**	11.8	**0.56**
21	6.29	11.42	**0.55**	12.42	0.51

The two extremes of tread length can be specified further:

The shortest tread comes for $N = 17$ steps, $R = 7.76$ inches. We can just set $\frac{R}{T} = 0.85$, the maximum allowed slope, and get $T \approx 9.13$ inches. As a check, $2R + T = 15.52 + 9.13 \approx 24.65$, which is less than the maximum of 25.

The longest tread comes for $N = 21$ steps, $R = 6.29$ inches. Here we can set $\frac{R}{T} = 0.55$, the minimum allowed slope, and get $T \approx 11.4$ inches.

Using this Task

If you are using this task as part of a formal system of assessment, it should be presented to students with standardized instructions. For such purposes give each student a copy of the task and remind them that today is an assessment of their individual work.

For informal classroom use, students may work in pairs or in groups. It would be useful to collate student responses in a table such as that shown on the previous page. Here students would have an excellent example of a task that has more than one correct answer.

Extensions

Designing a Staircase can be extended by asking students to generate a number of acceptable solutions. Students may want to explore the use of slope in the context of wheelchair access. The Balanced Assessment task *Wheelchair Access* (Task 6), invites students to create access in accordance with the regulations laid out in the *Americans with Disabilities Act*.

Task 4

Characterizing Performance

This section offers a characterization of student responses and provides indications of the ways in which the students were successful or unsuccessful in engaging with and completing the task. The descriptions are keyed to the *Core Elements of Performance*. Our global descriptions of student work range from "The student needs significant instruction" to "The student's work meets the essential demands of the task." Samples of student work that exemplify these descriptions of performance are included below, accompanied by commentary on central aspects of each student's response. These sample responses are *representative;* they may not mirror the global description of performance in all respects, being weaker in some and stronger in others.

The characterization of student responses for this task is based on these *Core Elements of Performance:*

1. Use the concept of slope (rise over run) in the setting of a staircase of repeated equal steps.
2. Work with inequalities that specify the minimum and maximum allowable slope.
3. Work with inequalities that specify minimum and maximum step size (where step size is measured as twice the rise plus the run).
4. Find the dimensions of a step that is within the guidelines and that can be used to span a given vertical distance.

Descriptions of Student Work

The student needs significant instruction.

Typically the student works in a way that is unsystematic and seemingly arbitrary. It is as if the student knows that the task entails some sort of manipulation, but is unclear as to the theory that might drive these manipulations.

Student A

This student shows that he knows how to convert feet to inches. This is a useful start, but it is not clear why the student starts with 17.6 steps.

The student needs some instruction.

Typically the student attempts to satisfy some but not all of the guidelines. The student focuses on one constraint, but the attempt is not sufficiently sustained to arrive at a specified model.

Student B

This student shows that she recognizes the importance of slope in this task. The student's approach to the problem is dominated by a search for a $\frac{rise}{run}$ that works. Notice the unequal equals that the student builds into her response when she writes something such as $\frac{55}{100} = \frac{85}{100}$. Setting the lower and upper values of the slope equal to each other is not helpful. It is almost as if the student hopes that setting up an "equation" might lead to possible values that will satisfy the constraints of the task. The procedure simply leads the student back to lower and upper values of slope. The student's response lies within the slope requirements but not within the second constraint, which has been ignored.

The student's work needs to be revised.

Aspects of the task are complete. The student typically proceeds by trial and error. This approach is quite time-consuming, but the student's attempt is sustained and delivers a possible solution. Typically the student does not show that each guideline has been met.

Student C

This student shows that she can use slope in a practical situation, but does not succeed in meeting each guideline. The student shows a consolidated understanding of slope. In addition, she shows that she makes a sustained attempt to meet each of the guidelines.

The student's work meets the essential demands of the task.

All core elements of performance are present. The student presents a design that is within each regulation. The student uses a diagram and explanations to show that each guideline is met.

Student D

This student shows that he can apply slope in a practical situation. The student figures out an accurate solution, and shows how each of the guidelines is met.

Staircase

11 feet X 12 inches = 132 inches

$$\frac{132 \text{ inches}}{17.6 \text{ steps}} = 7.5 \text{ inches each - tread}$$

The hight of the riser of each staircase will have to be 5.5 inches each and the

126 steps

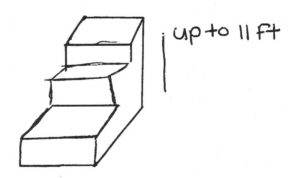

up to 11 ft

Student B

$$\frac{55}{100} = \frac{85}{100}$$

$$\frac{11}{20} = \frac{17}{20}$$

$$\frac{5.5}{10} = \frac{8.5}{10}$$

$$\frac{2.75}{5} = \frac{4.25}{5}$$

$$\frac{1.375}{2.5} = \frac{2.125}{2.5}$$

$$\frac{.55}{1} = \frac{0.85}{1}$$

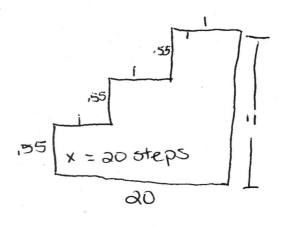

.55   x = 20 steps

20

total rise = 132 inch.

$\frac{rise}{run}$ = between .55 & .85

2 × rise + run = between 24 & 25 inch.

1) $\frac{total\ rise}{total\ run}$ = .55 $\frac{132}{y}$ = .55   y = 240 inches = total run

$\frac{132\ inch}{240\ inch}$ = $\frac{15}{27.2}$ 15×2 + 27.2 = 57.2 (too high)

$\frac{132}{240}$ = $\frac{4}{7.27}$ 4×2 + 7.27 = 15.3 (too low) $\frac{132}{240}$ = $\frac{8}{14.5}$ 8×2 + 14.5 = 30.5 (too high)

$\frac{132}{240}$ = $\frac{6}{10.9}$ 6×2 + 10.9 = 22.9 too low $\frac{132}{240}$ = $\frac{7}{12.7}$ 7×2 + 12.7 = 26.7 too high

$\frac{rise}{run}$ $\frac{132\ inch}{188.57\ inch}$ = .7 (slope) $\frac{132\ inch}{68.57\ inch}$ = $\frac{7\ inch}{10\ inch}$ 7(2)+10 = 24 inch.
yes between .55 - .85   yes (between 24 - 25 inch)

rise: height (rise) = 7 inch

tread length (run) = 10 inch

$\frac{132\ inch}{7\ inch}$ = almost 19 risers needed

$\frac{.132}{19}$ = 6.95 inch = rise $\frac{188.57\ inch}{10\ inch}$ = almost 19 treads needed

riser height (rise) = 6.95 inch. $\frac{188.57}{19}$ = 9.92 inch/tread

tread length (run) = 9.92 inch.

$\frac{6.95\ inch\ rise}{9.92\ inch\ run}$ = .7 = slope   yes between .55 & .85

6.95 ×2 + 9.92 = 23.8

NO (Not between 24 - 25!)

WRONG

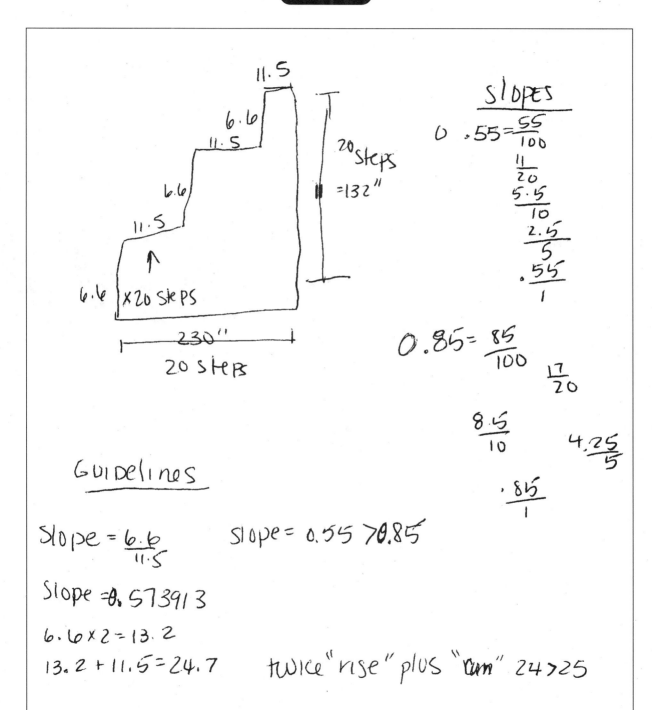

SLOPES

$0 \; .55 = \dfrac{55}{100}$

$\dfrac{11}{20}$

$\dfrac{5.5}{10}$

$\dfrac{2.5}{5}$

$\dfrac{.55}{1}$

$0.85 = \dfrac{85}{100}$

$\dfrac{17}{20}$

$\dfrac{8.5}{10}$

$\dfrac{4.25}{5}$

$\dfrac{.85}{1}$

11.5

6.6
11.5

6.6

11.5

6.6 x20 Steps

20 steps =132"

230"
20 steps

Guidelines

Slope = $\dfrac{6.6}{11.5}$ Slope = 0.55 > 0.85

Slope = 0.573913

6.6 × 2 = 13.2

13.2 + 11.5 = 24.7   twice "rise" plus "run" 24 > 25

5

Packaging a Soda Bottle

Measure accurately.

Draw nets of rectangular and hexagonal prisms.

Use the Pythagorean theorem or trigonometry to find the dimensions of the nets.

Estimate how many nets fit onto a piece of cardboard.

Justify computations.

Long Task

Task Description

In this task students are asked to sketch the net for two boxes, a rectangular solid and a hexagonal prism, including all the measurements. In the latter case, a scale drawing and the Pythagorean theorem or trigonometry are needed in order to calculate the dimensions.

Assumed Mathematical Background

It is assumed that students have experience of drawing nets of three-dimensional shapes, using the Pythagorean theorem or the trigonometric ratios.

Core Elements of Performance

- measure a drawing accurately in centimeters and millimeters
- use spatial visualization skills to draw nets
- visualize the way in which the nets will be glued together
- use the Pythagorean theorem or trigonometry in solving for the surface area of each net
- estimate the number of box nets that would fit onto a 1 m $\times$ 1 m piece of cardboard
- justify computations

Circumstances

Grouping:	Following work in pairs, students complete an individual written response.
Materials:	30-centimeter ruler, calculator, scissors (optional), and gluesticks (optional)
Estimated time:	60 minutes

Packaging a Soda Bottle

This problem gives you the chance to

- *measure accurately*
- *sketch the nets of 3-D shapes showing dimensions*
- *find the surface area of each net*
- *estimate how many nets can be cut from a piece of cardboard*
- *justify your computations*

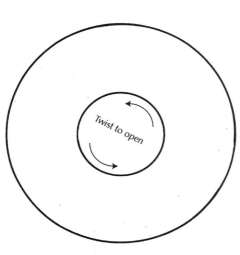

Twist to open

Mrs. Grundy wants to package bottles of her homemade cola in boxes.

An accurate full-size drawing of the top and side views of her bottle is shown.

There are two possible box designs she may use.

One has a square top and one has a hexagonal top.

These boxes must be a tight fit, or the bottles will rattle around when they are being transported.

Mrs. Grundy's Special Dandelion Cola

1. Sketch diagrams to show how you would make each box from a single piece of cardboard. You do not need to do this precisely.

   Show where you would put flaps for gluing each box together.

2. By measuring the drawing of the bottle in centimeters, figure out the length of *every* edge of each box in centimeters.

   Show how you figured out these lengths.

   On your diagrams for question 1, write down these lengths.

3. Calculate the amount of cardboard used by each design in square centimeters.

   Show how you figured this out.

4. Suppose you had a sheet of cardboard 1 meter long and 1 meter wide.

   Estimate the number of square-top boxes that could be made from a single sheet. Explain your reasoning.

   Estimate the number of hexagon-top boxes that could be made from a single sheet. Explain your reasoning.

Task **5**

A Sample Solution

The measurements in the following diagrams are given to the nearest millimeter.

They are the minimum measurements acceptable.

1. Measurements 1 mm greater than these are acceptable. Beyond that the bottle will tend to rattle around too much! The positions of the flaps for glue may be varied from those shown, but must be in sensible positions.

2. The calculation of the side of one hexagon may be done using a scale drawing, the Pythagorean theorem, or by trigonometry. It will result in a hexagon of side length $\sqrt{12}$ = 3.5 cm to the nearest mm.

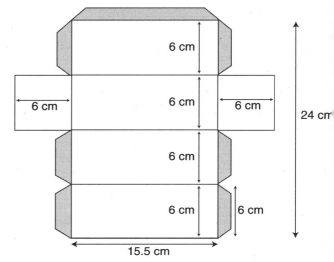

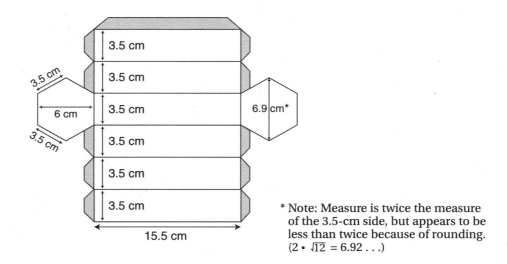

* Note: Measure is twice the measure of the 3.5-cm side, but appears to be less than twice because of rounding. $(2 \cdot \sqrt{12} = 6.92 \ldots)$

3. The area of cardboard needed for each design (excluding flaps) will be given by the formulas shown below:

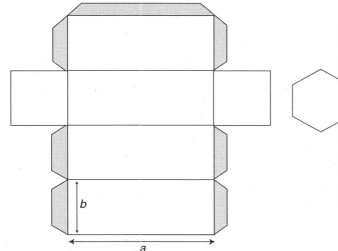

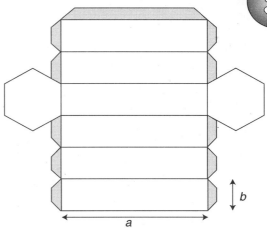

For the rectangular solid, the surface area $= 4ab + 2b^2 = 2b(2a + b)$.

For the hexagonal box, the surface area $= 6ab + 2\left(\frac{3\sqrt{3}}{2}b^2\right) = 3b(2a + \sqrt{3}b)$.

When evaluating, follow through the student's own measurements.

For the measurements on the previous page, the rectangular solid has a surface area of about 444 cm^2, while the hexagonal box has a surface area of about 389 cm^2.

4. A medium-level response to this task would just involve dividing the area of the sheet by the area of card used to give an estimate in each case. This may be an optimistic estimate; the nets, however, may not tessellate very well, particularly when the flaps are taken into account. A high-level response would mention this and might sketch the placement of the nets on the cardboard. In fact, the results with simple division are 22 rectangular and 25 hexagonal boxes. The actual results, assuming 1-cm flaps, are 14 rectangular and 16 hexagonal boxes.

Task

Using this Task

When introducing this task, emphasize the following points:

- students should measure the bottle in centimeters.

- accurate drawings are not required.

- students should explain their reasoning as carefully and as fully as possible.

Allow students to discuss their ideas with at most one partner; discourage pairs from sharing with other pairs.

If any students become completely stuck and need to make models in order to help them visualize the boxes, they may be allowed to do so. A supply of scissors and glue sticks should be made available for this purpose. Please make it clear to students, however, that the purpose of the task is not to assess model making or accurate drawing and they should not spend longer than is necessary on these activities. Also note that grid paper and geometric dot paper should not be issued, as these imply to students that accurate drawings should be made.

Characterizing Performance

This section offers a characterization of student responses and provides indications of the ways in which the students were successful or unsuccessful in engaging with and completing the task. The descriptions are keyed to the *Core Elements of Performance*. Our global descriptions of student work range from, "The student needs significant instruction" to "The student's work meets the essential demands of the task." Samples of student work that exemplify these descriptions of performance are included below, accompanied by commentary on central aspects of each student's response. These sample responses are *representative;* they may not mirror the global description of performance in all respects, being weaker in some and stronger in others.

The characterization of student responses for this task is based on these *Core Elements of Performance:*

1. Measure a drawing accurately in centimeters and millimeters.
2. Use spatial visualization skills to draw nets.
3. Visualize the way in which the nets will be glued together.
4. Use the Pythagorean theorem or trigonometry in solving for the surface area of each net.
5. Estimate the number of box nets that would fit onto a 1 m × 1 m piece of cardboard.
6. Justify computations.

Descriptions of Student Work

The student needs significant instruction.

These papers show evidence of clear understanding of the fact that they need to sketch nets of rectangular and hexagonal boxes, including flaps. Typically the sketches for both boxes may be correct, but the number or position of flaps may not be correct. The dimensions for the rectangular box may be correct, but the dimensions of the hexagonal box will be inaccurate.

Student A

Student A has drawn sketches of the nets of a rectangular and a hexagonal box. The dimensions of the rectangular box are correct, but an extra flap has been drawn: its surface area has been correctly calculated numerically, but the dimensions shown are linear as is the conversion from centimeters to meters. The dimensions of the sides of the hexagonal box are incorrect.

The student needs some instruction.

These papers provide evidence of a clear understanding that there is a need to sketch the nets of a rectangular and a hexagonal box, showing the appropriate dimensions, and calculating the amount of cardboard needed to make it.

Typically the dimensions of the rectangular box will be correct and the amount of cardboard needed to make this box may be correctly calculated. The dimensions of the hexagonal box, however, will be incorrect.

Student B

Student B has produced a correct net for the rectangular solid box, with flaps shown in suitable places. The net for the hexagonal box, however, is too large as the response assumed that each hexagon should have an edge of 6 cm.

The calculation for the area of cardboard used in the rectangular solid is again correct. The response did not calculate the area of a hexagonal face for the hexagon box.

Student B did not attempt question 4, presumably because the student thought that both of the nets had a larger area than 1 square meter. Looking at the answer to question 3, one can see that the student thinks that there are 100 square centimeters in a square meter.

The student's work needs to be revised.

These papers provide evidence of a clear understanding that there is a need to sketch the nets of a rectangular and a hexagonal box, showing the appropriate dimensions to calculate the amount of cardboard needed and estimating how many nets can be cut from a sheet of cardboard.

Typically the nets of both prisms are correctly drawn, including the flaps, and the dimensions of both boxes are correctly shown. (The Pythagorean theorem is used to find the dimensions of the hexagonal box.) The amount of cardboard needed to make each prism is calculated, but there may be minor errors. The number of nets that can be cut from a sheet of cardboard is calculated, but no allowance is made for cardboard wasted.

Student C

Student C has correctly drawn sketches of the nets of rectangular and a hexagonal boxes. The dimensions of both boxes are correct and the flaps are correct, if we find it acceptable to have only one flap on the top at the front edge. Although these nets are correct, they are not compact and could be very wasteful of cardboard.

The dimensions of the hexagon are correctly determined using the Pythagorean theorem, and the calculations of the amount of cardboard needed are correct. An estimate of the number of nets that can be made from a sheet of cardboard is made, but no allowance for waste is made: in this case, the estimate could be very inaccurate.

The student's work meets the essential demands of the task.

These papers provide evidence of a clear understanding that there is a need to sketch the nets of a rectangular and a hexagonal box, showing the appropriate dimensions to calculate the amount of cardboard needed and estimate how many nets can be cut from a sheet of cardboard.

Typically the nets of both boxes are correctly drawn, including flaps, and the dimensions of both boxes are correctly shown. (The Pythagorean theorem is used to find the dimensions of the hexagonal box.) The amount of cardboard needed to make each box is correctly calculated. The number of nets that can be cut from a sheet of cardboard is calculated and some allowance is made for cardboard wasted. Computations are justified.

Student D

This is a very good response. Student D has successfully designed the two nets, and has added the glue flaps in sensible places. For the "square top" net, some of these flaps are 3 cm wide, whereas elsewhere they are 1 cm wide. The necessary dimensions are all present. The response shows real ability at dealing with the dimensions of the hexagonal box, though some have been left as radicals.

The calculations for the area of cardboard are correct and these include the area of the glue flaps. The response has not evaluated the area of the hexagonal net for some reason. (Perhaps there was no calculator available?)

The solution to question 4 is well done. The response has calculated (correctly) the overall dimensions for each net, including the flaps and has then divided each dimension into 100 cm and rounded down. This approach is perhaps not the most efficient as it does not allow for any tessellation of the nets, but it shows a commendable clarity of thought.

Student A

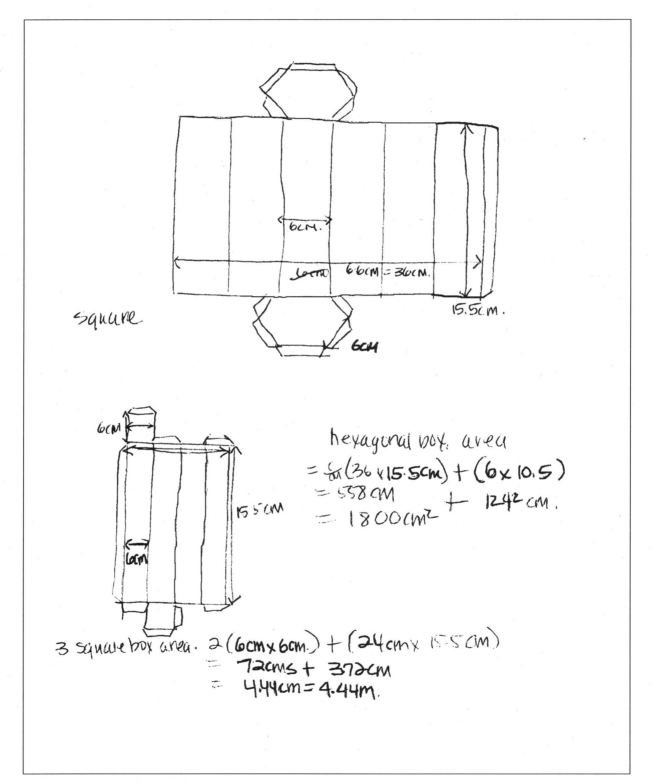

square

hexagonal box. area

$$= \frac{5}{6a}(36 \times 15.5cm) + (6 \times 10.5)$$
$$= 558 cm + 1242 cm.$$
$$= 1800 cm^2$$

3 square box area. $2(6cm \times 6cm.) + (24cm \times 15.5 cm)$
$$= 72cms + 372cm$$
$$= 444cm = 4.44m.$$

Student B

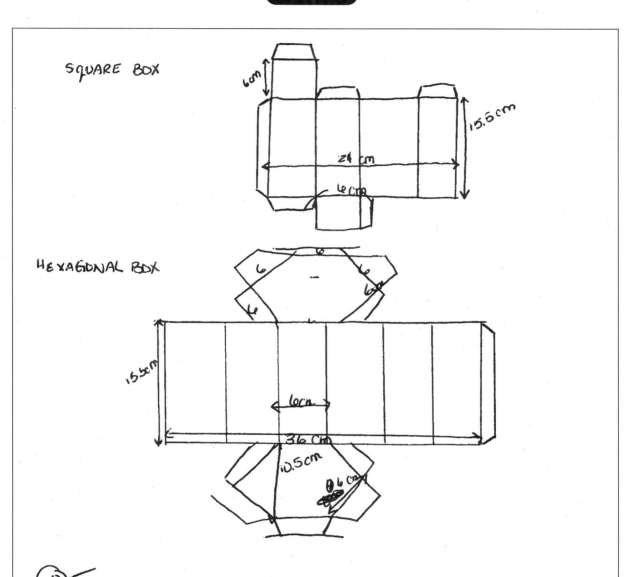

SQUARE BOX

6cm

15.5cm

24 cm

6 cm

HEXAGONAL BOX

6

8

6

6cm

6cm

15.5cm

6cm

36 Cm

10.5cm

θ 6 cm

②

③ SQUARE BOX area = $2(6cm \times 6cm) + (24cm \times 15.5cm)$ =
$$= 72 + 372$$
$$= 444 \ cm^2 - 4.44 m^2$$

Hexagonal box area = $(36 \times 15.5 cm) + (6 \times 10.5)2$ =
$$= 558 + 1242$$
$$= 1800 \ cm^2$$

Packaging at bottle in a box

1. Rectangular

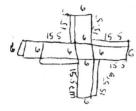

Hexagonal

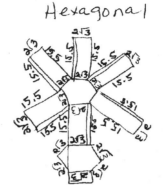

2. measure of heights 15.5 cm
measure of width: 6 cm

$(n-2)180$
$(6-2) \cdot 180 = 720$

$\dfrac{720}{6} = 120$

$\dfrac{3}{\sqrt{3}} \cdot = \sqrt{3}$

$\sqrt{3 \cdot 2} - 2\sqrt{3}$

3. We said each flap was 1cm wide.

"Square Top"
$15.5 \cdot 7 = 108.5$
$108.5 \cdot 4 = 434$
$6 \cdot 7 = 42$
$6 \cdot 6 = 36$
$434 + 42 + 36 = \boxed{512 \text{ cm}^2}$

Hexagonal Top
$15.5 \cdot 2\sqrt{3} = 31\sqrt{3}$
$31\sqrt{3} \cdot 6 = 186\sqrt{3}$
$15.5 \cdot 6 = 93$
$12\sqrt{3} + 12\sqrt{3} = 24\sqrt{3}$
$48\sqrt{3} + 2\sqrt{3}$

$\boxed{236\sqrt{3} + 93 \text{ cm}^2}$

4. $100 \, cm^2 = 10000 \, cm$

$\dfrac{10000}{512} = 19$

$\dfrac{10000}{501.76} \, 39906 = 19$

$\sqrt{3} \approx 1.73$

$1.73 \ast 236 = 408.28 + 93 = 501.28$

$\dfrac{10000}{501.28} = 19$

You have enough material to make 19 boxes for each of the shapes.

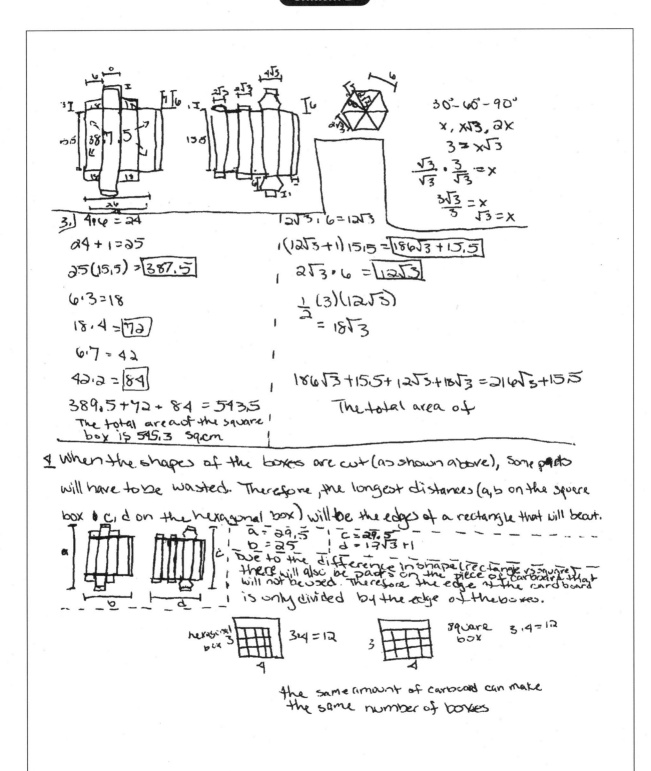

30°-60°-90°

x, x√3, 2x

3 = x√3

$\frac{\sqrt{3}}{\sqrt{3}} \cdot \frac{3}{\sqrt{3}} = x$

$\frac{3\sqrt{3}}{3} = x$ √3 = x

3.) 4•6 = 24

24 + 1 = 25

25(15,5) = 387.5

6•3 = 18

18•4 = 72

6•7 = 42

42•2 = 84

389.5 + 72 + 84 = 543.5
The total area of the square
box is 545.3 sq.cm

2√3•6 = 12√3

1(12√3 + 1) 15.5 = 186√3 + 15.5

2√3•6 = 12√3

$\frac{1}{2}$ (3)(12√3)
= 18√3

186√3 + 15.5 + 12√3 + 18√3 = 216√3 + 15.5
The total area of

4 When the shapes of the boxes are cut (as shown above), some parts will have to be wasted. Therefore, the longest distances (a,b on the square box & c,d on the hexagonal box) will be the edges of a rectangle that will bear.

a = 29.5   c = 29.5
b = 25   d = 17√3 + 1

Due to the difference in shape (rectangle vs square) there will also be parts on the piece of cardboard that will not be used. Therefore the edge of the cardboard is only divided by the edge of the boxes.

hexagonal box 3   3•4 = 12

square box 3   3•4 = 12

the same amount of cardboard can make the same number of boxes

6

Select and use the concept of slope. Interpret specifications.

Wheelchair Access

Long Task

Task Description

Students are told that wheelchair access is required for a viewing platform that is 10 feet high. The ramp must conform to the specifications of the *Americans with Disabilities Act*.

Assumed Mathematical Background

Students should have completed some work with the concept of slope thought of as the (vertical) rise divided by the (horizontal) run.

Core Elements of Performance

- use the concept of slope in the setting of a wheelchair ramp
- interpret the specifications and constraints of the *Americans with Disabilities Act*

Circumstances

Grouping:	Students complete an individual written response.
Materials:	rulers
Estimated time:	45 minutes

Wheelchair Access

This problem gives you the chance to

- *design a ramp to provide wheelchair access to a viewing platform, given the height of the platform and the requirements that all wheelchair ramps must meet*

Wheelchair access is needed for a viewing platform that is 10 feet above the ground. The ramp is to be built on a square area that has 45 feet on a side. The ramp must comply with the *Americans with Disabilities Act* specifications that are given below.

Draw a diagram to show how you have created the access.

Communicate your design decisions clearly: how many sections are there and what size are they?

Include your calculations.

Show how each specification is met.

The *Americans with Disabilities Act* specifications:

- The maximum slope that a wheelchair ramp can have is 1 in 12.
- No one section of the ramp can rise more than 30 inches.
- Higher rises are created by joining two sections with a horizontal landing that is at least 60 inches long.
- A ramp must have at least a 60-inch landing at the beginning and end.
- The width of a ramp must be 72 inches.*

*The actual ADA specifications call for a width of 36 in., but many manufacturers use 72 in. for ease in turning and passing.

A Sample Solution

Scale: $\frac{1}{4}$-inch represents 2 feet.

Total of five linked ramps.

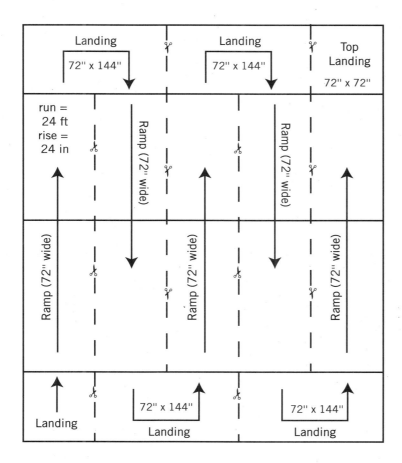

Task

Using this Task

Many students found this task challenging. Communicating the solution is one of its more challenging aspects. If at all possible, encourage students to make a model ramp as a solution, and this will give students a means to communicate effectively this complex structure. Useful materials that can be used to make a ramp are paper or cardboard.

Characterizing Performance

This section offers a characterization of student responses and provides indications of the ways in which the students were successful or unsuccessful in engaging with and completing the task. The descriptions are keyed to the *Core Elements of Performance.* Our global descriptions of student work range from "The student needs significant instruction" to "The student's work meets the essential demands of the task." Samples of student work that exemplify these descriptions of performance are included below, accompanied by commentary on central aspects of each student's response. These sample responses are *representative;* they may not mirror the global description of performance in all respects, being weaker in some and stronger in others.

The characterization of student responses for this task is based on these *Core Elements of Performance:*

1. Use the concept of slope in the setting of a wheelchair ramp.
2. Interpret the specifications and constraints of the *Americans with Disabilities Act.*

Descriptions of Student Work

The student needs significant instruction.

These papers show at most evidence that the student has a clear understanding of at least one of the constraints.

Student A

This response shows that the student formulates the problem as that of determining the number of 30-inch ramps needed to reach a height of 120 inches. The response does not show us that the student knows how to construct slopes that conform to the specifications of the ADA.

The student needs some instruction.

These papers provide evidence that the student has some understanding of slope.

Task

6

Student B

This response shows that the student can design a ramp with the required slope. The student has interpreted the constraints but has difficulty orienting the ramp so that it fits into the given space.

The student's work needs to be revised.

These papers show that the student has essentially accomplished the task. The work could be revised to perfection.

Student C

This student has difficulty communicating the work that has been carried out. The construction of a model would help the student to show how each of the constraints has been met.

The student's work meets the essential demands of the task.

The student ensures that each constraint is met and fully accomplishes the task.

Student D

This response presents a model that is made with paper. The darker lines indicate where the paper has been cut to make a model ramp.

Wheel Chair

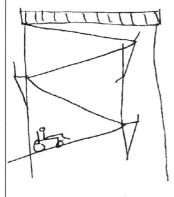

45' wide or 540"

4/30 inches high raMPs
Connected to 5
Plat Forms to 60 inches
long

40 RaMPs altogether
30$\overline{)120}$ inches high
inch's
RISing.

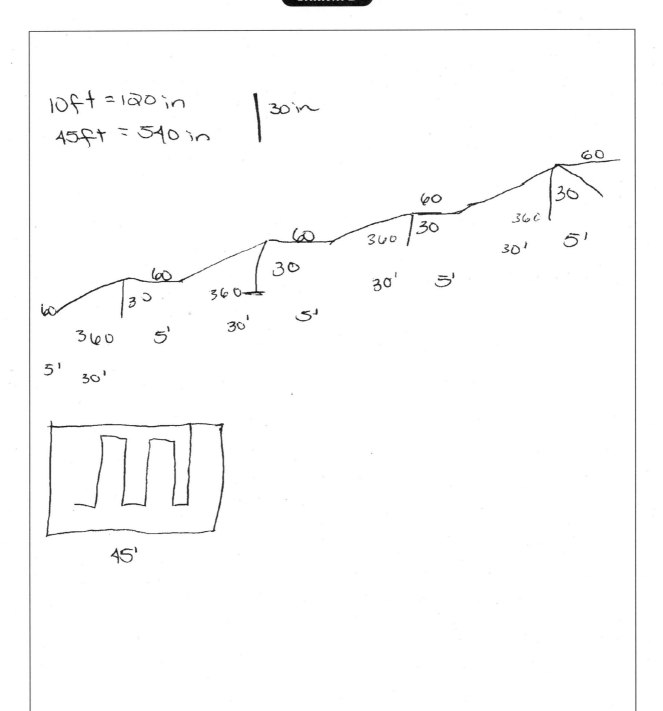

10ft = 120in
45ft = 540in

30in

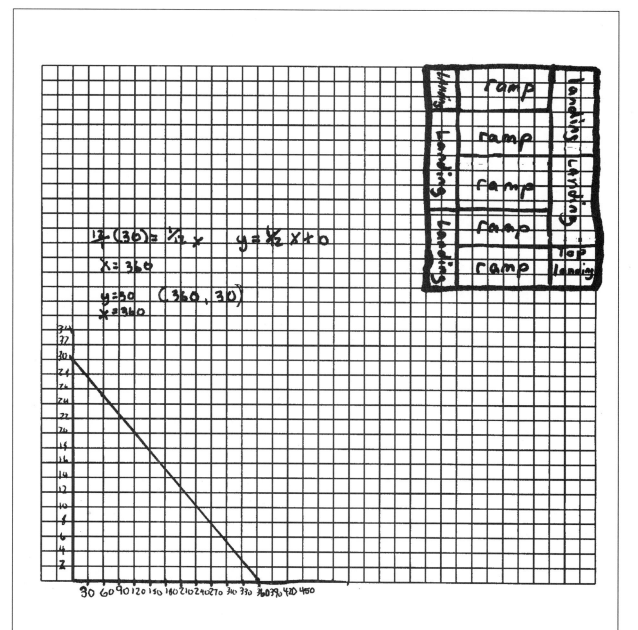

$\frac{1}{2}(36) = \frac{1}{12}x \qquad y = \frac{1}{12}x + 0$

$x = 360$

$y = 30 \qquad (360, 30)$
$x = 360$

Student D

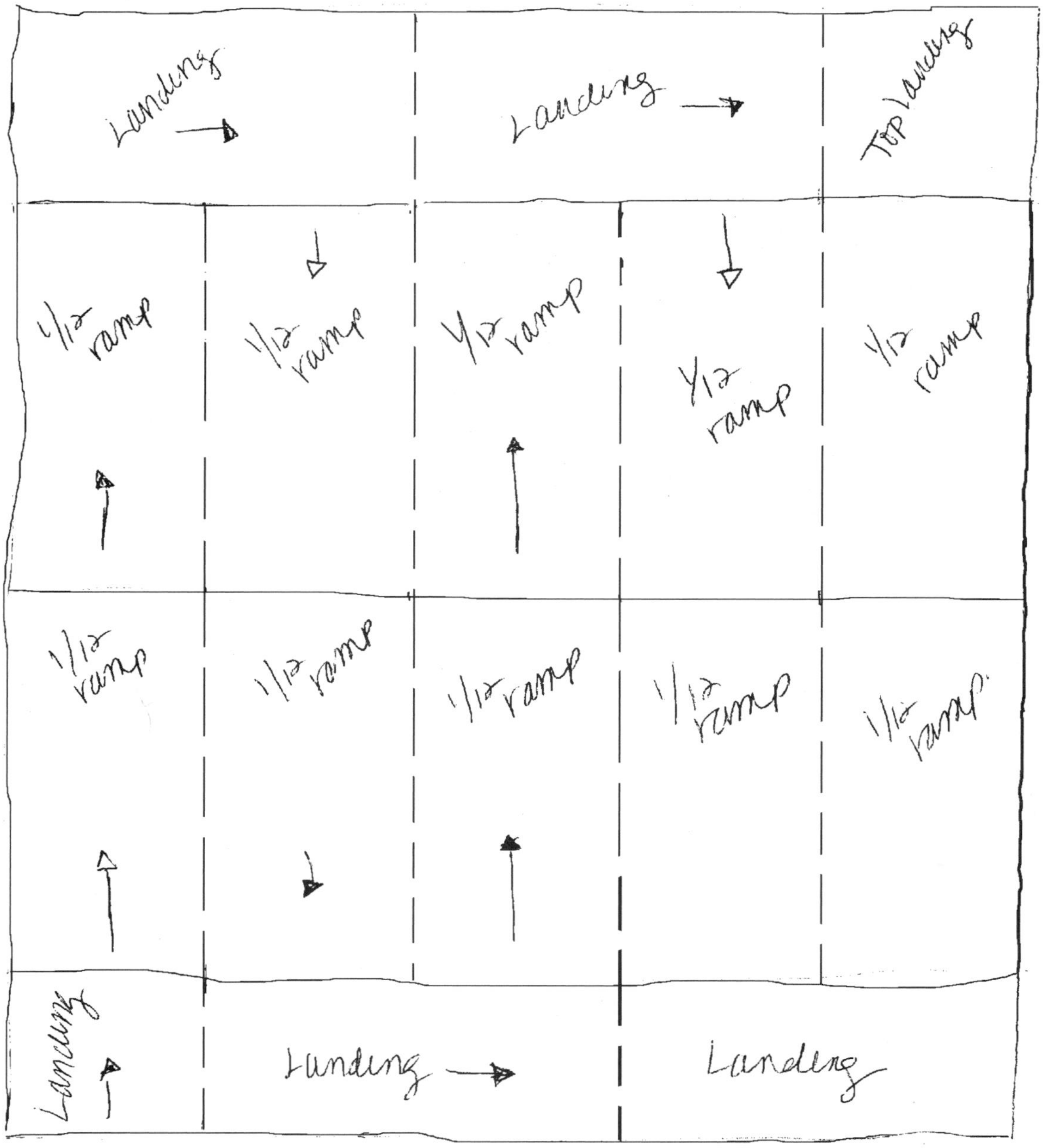
Landing
Landing
Top Landing
1/12 ramp
1/12 ramp
1/12 ramp
1/12 ramp
1/12 ramp
1/12 ramp
1/12 ramp
1/12 ramp
1/12 ramp
1/12 ramp
Landing
Landing
Landing

Kidney Stones

Interpret a statement from an article in a health newsletter.

Answer questions about proportions given information in the article.

Distinguish part-part and part-whole relationships.

Long Task

Task Description

This task starts by showing part of an article that gives both the proportion of Americans who have a certain disease and the proportion of Americans with this disease who are men. The task then asks students to show how these two proportions interact to give the proportion of American men with the disease, and the proportion of American women with the disease.

Assumed Mathematical Background

Students should have had some experience working with parts of a whole expressed as proportions.

Core Elements of Performance

- work with parts of a whole expressed as proportions
- deal with three kinds of cases
    — cases in which two proportions need to be multiplied
    — cases in which two proportions need to be added or subtracted
    — cases in which two proportions need to be divided
- represent parts of a whole as circle graphs
- generalize a situation using symbols instead of specific numbers

Circumstances

Grouping:	Following work in pairs, students complete an individual written response.
Materials:	grid paper, ruler, protractor, and calculator
Estimated time:	45 minutes

Acknowledgments

The data in this task are reprinted from the University of California, Berkeley Wellness Letter, August 1993.

Kidney Stones

This problem gives you the chance to

- *interpret information from an article*
- *use given information about proportions to find other information*

This statement appeared in a newsletter on health:

About one in ten Americans eventually develop a kidney stone.
Four out of five stone formers are men.

People who develop a kidney stone are called "stone formers." In terms of proportions, the newsletter says that:
- The proportion of Americans who are stone formers is **0.1**.
- The proportion of stone formers who are men is **0.8**.

1. **a.** What proportion of American **men** eventually develop a kidney stone?
   b. What proportion of American **women** eventually develop a kidney stone?
Show how you arrived at your answers. (You may assume that half of all Americans are men.)

Problem 1 is the heart of this task. Related problems appear on the following page. If you have trouble with problem 1, start to work problems 2 and 3 first. This will help with problem 1.

2. What proportion of Americans are
   a. men who eventually develop a kidney stone?
   b. men who never develop a kidney stone?
   c. women who eventually develop a kidney stone?
   d. women who never develop a kidney stone?
   Explain your reasoning. (You may assume that half of all Americans
   are men.)

3. What should the four proportions in problem 2 add up to, and why?
   Draw an accurate circle graph that illustrates these four categories.

Extension
   Suppose that a proportion *p* of Americans eventually develop heart
   disease, and that a proportion *q* of heart disease patients are men.

4. In terms of *p* and *q*,
   a. what proportion of American men eventually develop heart disease?
   b. what proportion of American women eventually develop heart
      disease?
   (In working this problem, think about how you answered problem 1 on
   the previous page.)

5. In terms of *p* and *q*, say what proportion of Americans are
   a. men who eventually develop heart disease.
   b. men who never develop heart disease.
   c. women who eventually develop heart disease.
   d. women who never develop heart disease.
   Do these proportions add up to the right number?
   (In working this problem, think about how you answered problem 2.)

6. Check your answers in problems 4 and 5 by substituting the numbers
   from the first part of this task and seeing if you get the same results.

Task **A Sample Solution**

1a. The answer is **0.16**.

Here is a way to think about this. Take a typical 100 Americans. Of these, 10 are stone formers (one out of ten Americans is a stone former). Of the 10 stone formers, 8 are men (four out of five stone formers are men). But also, out of these 100 Americans, 50 are men. This means that 8 out of these 50 men are stone formers. Since this selection is typical, $\frac{8}{50}$ or **0.16** of American men are stone formers.

In effect, this thinking involves taking a **ratio** of two **proportions**:

$$\frac{\text{proportion of stone formers who are men}}{\text{proportion of Americans who are men}} = \frac{0.08}{0.5} = 0.16$$

1b. The answer is **0.04**. The same reasoning is used:

$$\frac{\text{proportion of stone formers who are women}}{\text{proportion of Americans who are women}} = \frac{0.02}{0.5} = 0.04$$

2a. Since a proportion 0.1 of all Americans is a stone former, and a proportion 0.8 of stone formers are men, then a proportion $(0.1)(0.8) = \mathbf{0.08}$ of Americans are male stone formers.
These **proportions** are multiplied, since the second proportion 0.8 is part of the group (stone formers) identified in the first proportion.

2b. Assuming that a proportion 0.5 of Americans are men, it follows from 2a that a proportion 0.5 – 0.08 = **0.42** of Americans are male non-stone formers. The important relation here is

0.5 = 0.08 + 0.42

men = male stone formers + male nonstone formers
In this relation the proportions are added, and not multiplied as in 2a. This is because the proportion 0.08 of Americans who are male stone formers and the proportion 0.42 of Americans who are male nonstone formers are disjoint classes, as opposed to having one a part of the other. Their sum is 0.5 since together they comprise all American men.

2c. Similar reasoning to that of 2a can be used for women: Since a proportion 0.1 of all Americans are stone formers, and a proportion 0.2 of stone formers are women, then a proportion $(0.1)(0.2) = \mathbf{0.02}$ of Americans are female stone formers. And another approach: Since a proportion 0.1 of all Americans are stone formers, and a proportion **0.08** are *male* stone formers (2a), it follows that 0.1 – 0.08 = **0.02** are female stone formers.

Task

7

2d. Assuming that a proportion 0.5 of Americans are women, then a pr portion 0.5 – 0.02 = **0.48** of Americans are female nonstone formers.

3. These four proportions, 0.08, 0.42, 0.02, and 0.48, have a sum of 1. (Expressed as percentages they would have a sum of 100.) This is as expected, since together they represent **all** Americans, and they divide all Americans into four disjoint categories.

Here is a circle graph representing the situation.

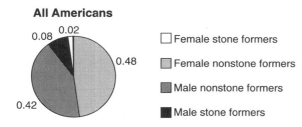

All Americans

☐ Female stone formers
▨ Female nonstone formers
▦ Male nonstone formers
■ Male stone formers

This particular chart shows all males on the left and all females on the right.

The number of degrees in each slice is needed for an accurate circle graph constructed with a protractor. The number of degrees is found by multiplying the proportion by 360°. These numbers are

$$(0.08)(360°) = 28.8° \qquad (0.02)(360°) = 7.2°$$
$$(0.42)(360°) = 151.2° \qquad (0.48)(360°) = 172.8°$$

Extension

4a. Using the reasoning of problem 1:

a proportion $\frac{pq}{0.5} = 2pq$ of American men eventually develops heart disease.

4b. Using the reasoning of problem 1:

a proportion $\frac{p(1-q)}{0.5} = 2p(1-q)$ of American women eventually develops heart disease.

5a. Using the reasoning of problem 2:
For men: A proportion p of Americans develop heart disease, and a proportion q of these are men. Therefore, a proportion pq of Americans are heart-disease males.

5b. Using the reasoning of problem 2:
Of the proportion 0.5 of Americans who are men, a proportion pq are heart-disease males, so a proportion **0.5 – pq** are nonheart-disease males.

Task

5c. Using the reasoning of problem 2:
For women: A proportion q of heart-disease Americans are men, which means that a proportion $1 - q$ of heart-disease Americans must be women. This in turn means that a proportion $p(1 - q)$ of Americans are heart-disease females.

5d. Using the reasoning of problem 2:
Of the proportion 0.5 of Americans who are women, a proportion $p(1 - q)$ are heart-disease females. It follows that a proportion $0.5 - p(1 - q)$ of Americans are nonheart-disease females.

Summarizing: Of all Americans, a proportion:
  a. pq are men who eventually develop heart disease.
  b. $0.5 - pq$ are men who never develop heart disease.
  c. $p(1 - q)$ are women who eventually develop heart disease.
  d. $0.5 - p(1 - q)$ are women who never develop heart disease.
Regardless of what p and q are, the algebraic sum of all these proportions is the number 1. This is as it should be, since all Americans fall into one or another of these 4 categories. (Expressed as percentages, all these
proportions would be multiplied by 100, and their algebraic sum would be 100.)

6. For the kidney stone disease, we have $p = 0.1$, $q = 0.8$.

4a.	$2pq$	$= 2(0.1)(0.8)$	$= 0.16$
4b.	$2p(1 - q)$	$= 2(0.1)(0.2)$	$= 0.04$
5a.	pq	$= (0.1)(0.8)$	$= 0.08$
5b.	$0.5 - pq$	$= 0.5 - (0.1)(0.8)$	$= 0.42$
5c.	$p(1 - q)$	$= (0.1)(1 - 0.8)$	$= 0.02$
5d.	$0.5 - p(1 - q)$	$= 0.5 - (0.1)(1 - 0.8)$	$= 0.48$

Using this Task

This task deals with proportions of Americans who have a certain disease. The article says,

> "About one in ten Americans eventually develop a kidney stone. Four out of five stone formers are men."

Remind students that proportions are simply ways of expressing parts of a whole. Any proportion can be expressed as a decimal, or as a fraction, or as a percent. For example, the proportion "four out of five" can be expressed in any of these forms:

$$0.8 \qquad \frac{4}{5} \qquad \frac{8}{10} \qquad 80\%$$

The intent behind this task is to see how well students understand typical ways of presenting information about proportions that are used in books, newspapers, and magazines.

Specifically, we are interested in seeing whether students understand, at least intuitively:

- that when two proportions each refer to parts of the same whole, then taking the **ratio** of the proportions shows what proportion the first part is of the second part (problem 1).

- that when one proportion refers to a part of a whole, and another proportion refers to a part of the first part, then **multiplying** the two proportions gives the proportion of the smaller part to the whole (problems 2a and 2c).

- that when two proportions refer to separate parts of a whole, then **adding** the two proportions gives the proportion of both parts together to the whole (problem 2b and 2d).

Note: In this task the term *proportion* is used in the way it is used in the real world. A proportion of a quantity means a definite part or fraction of the quantity; it can be expressed as a number between 0 and 1 (or as a percent between 0 and 100). Many school texts in this country have adopted a definition of proportion based on the classical Greek theory of proportion, namely a *proportion is a statement of equality between two ratios.* This meaning of proportion rarely appears outside a school text context.

In the last part (problems 4 and 5), we go on to see if students can generalize some of what they know using symbols like p and q instead of specific numbers to stand for proportions.

Task 7

Characterizing Performance

This section offers a characterization of student responses and provides indications of the ways in which the students were successful or unsuccessful in engaging with and completing the task. The descriptions are keyed to the *Core Elements of Performance*. Our global descriptions of student work range from "The student needs significant instruction" to "The student's work meets the essential demands of the task." Samples of student work that exemplify these descriptions of performance are included below, accompanied by commentary on central aspects of each student's response. These sample responses are *representative;* they may not mirror the global description of performance in all respects, being weaker in some and stronger in others.

The characterization of student responses for this task is based on these *Core Elements of Performance:*

1. Work with parts of a whole expressed as proportions.
2. Deal with three kinds of cases
   — cases in which two proportions need to be multiplied.
   — cases in which two proportions need to be added or subtracted.
   — cases in which two proportions need to be divided.
3. Represent parts of a whole as circle graphs.
4. Generalize a situation using symbols instead of specific numbers.

Descriptions of Student Work

The student needs significant instruction.

These papers show, at most, evidence that the student can conceptualize the situation in terms of an example: thinking in terms of an average 100 Americans.

Student A

This response states correctly in question 1a that 8 out of 100 Americans are male stone formers, but then goes on to state incorrectly that 8 out of 100 American men are stone formers. This amounts to using an incorrect "whole" for this "part-whole" situation. The rest of the response is incomplete or incorrect.

The student needs some instruction.

These papers provide evidence of multiplication of two proportions to arrive at a proportion representing "a part of a part."

Student B

The response clearly labels each proportion used, but fails to keep clear what the relevant "whole" is in the various part-whole situation.

The student's work needs to be revised.

These papers show correct answers for the numerical problems, and have at least minimal explanations. They make some headway on the problems requiring generalization in terms of p and q, but they don't get them fully correct.

Student C

This student correctly answers problems 1–3, but the explanations are skimpy and for some reason the student illustrates a circle graph using numbers that are different from those found in his correct solution to problem 2. The work presented for problems 4 and 5 is not quite right and needs to be revised.

The student's work meets the essential demands of the task.

Typically, these papers may have a few flaws.

Student D

This response is a strong one. The weakest point is the circle graph.

STAR QUALITY

Student E
This response is concise, correct, clear, and insightful in its explanation. It also has an elegant circle graph.

Kidney Stone

American stone formers = 0.1
Stone formers who are men = 0.8

Problem 1
   a) Amer. men who develop a Kidney stone =
     1) Out of 100 0.1 Americans form a Stone = 10
     2) out of the 0.8 = 8
     3 8:100 American Men Form Kidney stones = 4:50 2:25

   b) Amer. Women who develop a Kidney stone =
     1) .8 men out of 10 leaves 2 women 2:10 1/5

2) .1 form Kidney ston .8 of those are men = $\frac{.1}{.8}$

   b) ~~.8 .8:2~~ $\frac{.1}{.2}$
   c) $\frac{.1}{.2}$
   d) $\frac{.1}{.8}$

3) They should add up to **2** = 100%

4) $\frac{p}{q}$ = ~~scribble~~

   b) ~~scribble~~ $p - \frac{p}{q}$

5) where m = # of men $\frac{p}{q}$ > m =

1a. The proporation of stone formers who are American men one is .08 american stone formers → (.1)(.8) = .08
   men ↑ stone formers

b. The proporation of American women who are stone formers is .02 (.1)(.2) = .02

2a. The proporation of Americans who are male stone formers is .04 American stone formers → (.1)(.5)(.8) = .04
   1/2 americans are men ↑ male stone formers

b. The proporation of Americans who are men and Never form a stone is .46 Americans who are men (.5) - (.04) = .46
   The men who form a stone ↑

c. The proporation of Americans who are women and stone formers is .01 women (.5)(.1)(.2) = .0₂
   american stone formers ↑ women stone formers

d. The proporation of Americans who are women and Never form a stone is .49
   → (.5) - (.0₂) = .49
   1/2 American's are female ↑   # of Americans female stone formers

3. Because we started with americans as a whole and then broke it down into four categories

   SF = Stone Former
   N = Not a stone formers

4A (p)(q)
 b (p)(1-q)
5a (.5)(p)(q)
 b (.5) - ((.5)(p)(q))
 c (.5)(p)(1-q)
 d (.5) - [(.5)(p)(1-q)]
6. They work!

① a) .16

b) .04
Ten in every hundred (given)

men 50, 8 amount of men in a hundred
women 50 2 amount of women in a hundred

$\frac{8}{50}$ $\frac{2}{50}$

.16 .04

  ⎧ Proportion of women with stones
  ⎩ Proportion of men with stones

② a) .08 same as #1 excep
  b) .42 ÷ by 100 total
  c) .02 Americans
  d) .48

Stone growers

③ 1 = 100% of Americans

④ a. 9/50
  b. p-9/ 50

⑤ a 9/100
  b (50-9) /100
  c p-9 /100
  d [50-(p-9)] /100

Same as #2
more algebra because
there are no numbers

Student D

About one in 10 Americans eventually develop a kidney stone.
Four out of five stone formers are men.

People who develop a kidney stone are called "stone formers." In terms of
proportions, the newsletter says that:
■ The proportion of Americans who are stone formers is 0.1.
■ The proportion of stone formers who are men is 0.8.

1. a. What proportion of American **men** eventually develop a kidney stone?
   b. What proportion of American **women** eventually develop a kidney stone?
Show how you arrived at your answers. (You may assume that half of all
Americans are men.)

Problem 1 is the heart of this task. Related problems appear on the following
page. If you have trouble with problem 1, start to work problems 2 and 3 first.
This will help with problem 1.

a. 16% of American men are stone formers because 8% of all
Americans are men who develop them and only half
of all Americans are men. So, the amount of men who
develop them is 2(8%) or 16%.

b. 4% of all American women develop kidney
stones for the same reasons as above.

2. What proportion of Americans are
   a. men who eventually develop a kidney stone? 8%
   b. men who never develop a kidney stone? 42%
   c. women who eventually develop a kidney stone? 2%
   d. women who never develop a kidney stone? 48%
   Explain your reasoning. (You may assume that half of all Americans
   are men.) The reason these are exactly half of the amount in the
   previous problem is because the percentages are taken of all Americans +
3. What should the four proportions in problem 2 add up to, and why? are not split up
   Draw an accurate circle graph that illustrates these four categories. into gender.
   The four proportions should, and do, add up to 100%, because they

   Extension represent the 4 portions (that are relevant to the problem) of the entire
   Suppose that a proportion p of Americans eventually develop heart population
   disease, and that a proportion q of heart disease patients are men.

■ Stone formers
□ Non formers

42%   48%

8%:   2%

4. In terms of p and q,
   a. what proportion of American men eventually develop heart disease? $2pq$
   b. what proportion of American women eventually develop heart
      disease? $2p(1-q)$
   (In working this problem, think about how you answered problem 1 on
   the previous page.)

5. In terms of p and q, say what proportion of Americans are
   a. men who eventually develop heart disease. pq
   b. men who never develop heart disease. $50\% - pq$
   c. women who eventually develop heart disease. $p(1-q)$
   d. women who never develop heart disease. $50\% - p(1-q)$
   Do these proportions add up to the right number?
   (In working this problem, think about how you answered problem 2.)

6. Check your answers in problems 4 and 5 by substituting the numbers
   from the first part of this task and seeing if you get the same results.
   The results are all the same. It makes
   perfect sense because they are the same questions
   except for one set is algebraic and the other is numeric.

1. a) 16% ——⟶ .1
   b) 4% ——⟶ X.8
                  .08 of Americans are men X2 =.16 men who
                                                   have stones

2. a) 8%
   b) 42%
   c) 2%
   d) 48%

The percentage of men with stones is twice as much as the percentage of Americans who are male "stone formers", because of my assumption that there are equal numbers of men as woman. All that is left to do is to subtract the percentage from 50 (half the population) to get each non-stone-forming group.

4 a) 2 pq
   b) 2 [p - (pq)]

5 a) pq   ⟹   pq + [.50 - pq] + [p - pq] + [50 - {p - (pq)}]
   b) .50 - (pq)
   c) p - (pq)   [1]
   d) .50 - [p - (pq)]   yes, these proportions add up
                          to the right number. (1)

3. These four proportions should add up to 100%, the total American poplation.

Task **8**

Overview

Work from a map drawn to scale.

Use a rate to convert back and forth between distances and times.

Reason about distances using perpendicular bisectors and circles.

Lightning

Short Task

Task Description

Students are given maps showing the location of several people in relation to a place where lightning has struck. They are told that sound travels 1 kilometer in 3 seconds. The scale of the maps is 1 cm:1 km.

They are then are asked to reason about four different situations, and answer questions about the distances of the lightning compared to the time the thunder is heard.

Assumed Mathematical Background

Students need to have worked with scale drawings and maps. They also should have done some work in geometry with lines, perpendicular bisectors, and circles.

Core Elements of Performance

- make measurements from a map and convert these to real distances (using the given scale of the map)
- convert back and forth between distances and times, given a constant rate
- find and reason about the set of all points that are equidistant from two given points (perpendicular bisector)
- find and reason about the set of all points that are a fixed distance from a given point (circle)

Circumstances

Grouping:	Students complete an individual written response.
Materials:	ruler, compass, and calculator
Estimated time:	15 minutes

Lightning

107

Lightning

This problem gives you the chance to

- *solve problems about real situations involving lightning and thunder*
- *work from a map drawn to scale*
- *use ideas from geometry to reason about distances*

In a thunderstorm, you see the lightning before you hear the thunder.

This is because the light travels essentially instantaneously, whereas the sound of the thunder may take a few seconds to reach you.

One way to estimate the distance from where you are to where the lightning strikes is to count the number of seconds until you hear the thunder, and then divide that number by three. The number you get is the approximate distance in kilometers.

1. Suppose you see a lightning flash, and count 3 seconds before you hear the thunder.
   a. How far away was the lightning?

   b. What does the "divide by three" rule tell you about how fast the sound of thunder travels through the air? Explain.

2. People are standing at the four points *P, Q, R,* and *S* marked in the map below. They all saw lightning strike at point *L.*

Q

P

R

L (lightning)

S

Scale: 1 cm = 1 km

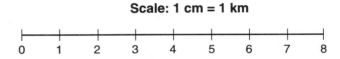

a. Who heard the thunder first? Why?

b. Who heard it last? Why?

c. One of the people heard it after about 15 seconds. Who was it? Explain.

d. After how many seconds did the person at *P* hear the thunder? Show how you know.

3. Now suppose lightning strikes again at a different place. The person at *P* and the person at *Q* both heard the thunder after the same amount of time.

  a. Show on the map below a place where the lightning might have struck.

  b. Are there other places where the lightning might have struck? If so, show as many of these places as you can.

  c. Can you tell which of *P* and *R* heard the thunder first? If so, explain how you know. If not, say why not.

Q ■

P ■

R ■

■ *S*

Scale: 1 cm = 1 km

0   1   2   3   4   5   6   7   8

4. Now suppose lightning strikes once again at yet a different place.
   a. If you know that the person at *P* heard the thunder 9 seconds after she saw the lightning, show on the map as many points as you can where the lightning might have struck.

   b. If you learn that the person at *R* heard the thunder from this same lightning stroke 18 seconds after he saw the lightning, show on the map the places where the lightning might have struck.

Q ■

P
■

R
■

■
S

Scale: 1 cm = 1 km

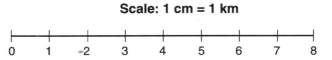

Task

A Sample Solution

1a. Using the given rule, 3 seconds divided by 3 is 1, so the distance is 1 kilometer.

1b. The "divide by three" rule says that sound travels 1 kilometer in 3 seconds. This is equivalent to 20 kilometers in 1 minute, or 1,200 kilometers per hour.

Measuring shows these approximate distances (in centimeters on the map, in kilometers in the real situation): $LP = 4.85$, $LQ = 5.0$, $LR = 5.6$, $LS = 6.5$

2a. P heard the thunder first, since P is closest to L.

2b. S heard it last, since S is farthest from L.

2c. Since $15 \div 3 = 5$, a person hearing thunder after 15 seconds should be 5 km away. This person is probably Q or P.

2d. Since the person at P is 4.85 km away, by the rule, P should hear the thunder $(3)(4.85) = 14.55$ seconds after the lightning. (15 seconds is acceptable.)

The set of all points equidistant from two given points is the perpendicular bisector of the line joining the two points. This fact is useful in answering these questions.

3a. A place where the lightning might have struck is halfway between P and Q.

3b. All other points on the perpendicular bisector m of $\overleftrightarrow{PQ}$ are also equidistant from P and Q, and so any point on m might have been where the lightning struck.

3c. No. Some points on m are closer to R than to P (and would be places where lightning would be heard by R first), while other points on m are closer to P than to R (and would be places where lightning would be heard by P first). Since the perpendicular bisector n of the line $\overleftrightarrow{PR}$ represents all points the same distance from P and R, the place where n and m cross is the dividing line between the P-hears-first and the R-hears-first locations on m.

A circle represents all the points a given distance from the center.

4a. If *P* hears the thunder after 9 seconds, *L* must be 3 km away from *P*. All such points form a circle of radius 3 cm centered at *P*.

4b. If *R* hears the thunder after 18 seconds, *L* must be 6 km away from *R*. All such points form a circle of radius 6 cm centered at *R*. These two circles intersect in two points, as can be seen from a drawing. The lightning must have struck at one of those two points.

Task

8

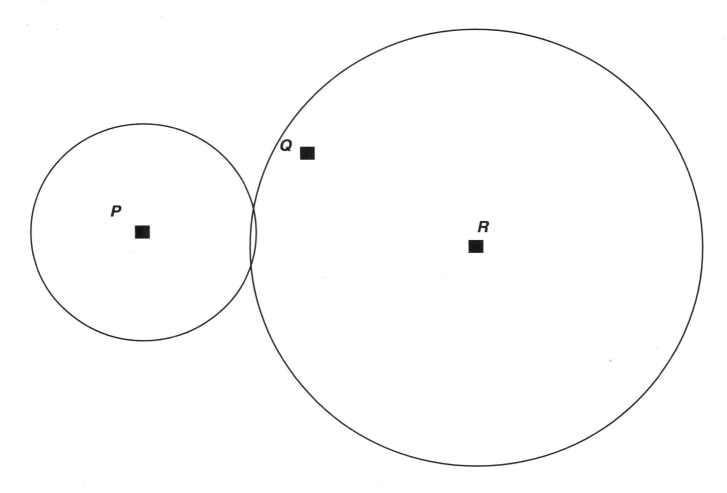

Task

Characterizing Performance

This section offers a characterization of student responses and provides indications of the ways in which the students were successful or unsuccessful in engaging with and completing the task. The descriptions are keyed to the *Core Elements of Performance*. Our global descriptions of student work range from "The student needs significant instruction" to "The student's work meets the essential demands of the task." Samples of student work that exemplify these descriptions of performance are included below, accompanied by commentary on central aspects of each student's response. These sample responses are *representative;* they may not mirror the global description of performance in all respects, being weaker in some and stronger in others.

The characterization of student responses for this task is based on these *Core Elements of Performance:*

1. Make measurements from a map and convert these to real distances (using the given scale of the map).
2. Convert back and forth between distances and times, given a constant rate.
3. Find and reason about the set of all points that are equidistant from two given points (perpendicular bisector).
4. Find and reason about the set of all points that are a fixed distance from a given point (circle).

Descriptions of Student Work

The student needs significant instruction.

These papers show at most some piece of work that could form part of a solution.

Student A

This response shows, in question 3, a correct placing of one point midway between *P* and *Q*. The other aspects of the response show an absence of understanding.

The student needs some instruction.

These papers show some understanding of some parts of the task, but there are some key ideas missing.

Typically there may be some appreciation of the speed and distance relation, but the notion of a set of points representing possible places for the lightning strike (and/or the fact that these are on a perpendicular bisector or a circle) is missing.

Student B

This response fails to explain the divide-by-three rule and makes three errors in stating the first and last hearers in question 2. In question 3, there is a single correct point shown with no other possibilities, and the answer to 3c is incorrect. In question 4, no sets of possible places are shown, but there is one point marked, and it is plausibly one of the possible correct positions, though there is no indicated justification for this.

The student's work needs to be revised.

These papers show appropriate strategies and substantially correct results, with possibly some minor errors or gaps. Typically, these will be in later parts.

Student C

This response shows a faulty explanation of the divide-by-three rule, but correct speed and distance calculations in question 2, except for rather rough distance measurements. The points marked in question 3 are only roughly in the right places, and there is no indication of a definite line, or of its being a perpendicular bisector. But the uncertainty about whether P or R will hear first is correctly noted. Question 4 shows a correct circular locus, and two correct points marked on it; this is essentially a correct and complete answer to the part.

The student's work meets the essential demands of the task.

These papers show a fully correct response, with appropriate explanations.

Student D

This response is full and correct, and well explained. The only omissions are the incorrect response to 3c and the failure to state that the points of intersection in question 4 are the points required.

Student A

Lightning

This problem gives you the chance to

- *solve problems about real situations involving lightning and thunder*
- *work from a map drawn to scale*
- *use ideas from geometry to reason about distances*

In a thunderstorm, you see the lightning before you hear the thunder.

This is because the light travels essentially instantaneously, whereas the sound of the thunder may take a few seconds to reach you.

One way to estimate the distance from where you are to where the lightning strikes is to count the number of seconds until you hear the thunder, and then divide that number by three. The number you get is the approximate distance in kilometers.

1. Suppose you see a lightning flash, and count 3 seconds before you hear the thunder.
   a. How far away was the lightning?

   3 Miles away

   b. What does the "divide by three" rule tell you about how fast the sound of thunder travels through the air? Explain.

   This means that FOR Every Second that lightning is countable 1 Mile = 1 Second 1 + 1 + 1 = 3 Miles Away. I learned this At A young age and it has stuck with me Eversince.

Student A

2. People are standing at the four points *P, Q, R,* and *S* marked in the map below. They all saw lightning strike at point *L*.

Q ■

P
■

R
■

■

L (lightning)

■
S

Scale: 1 cm = 1 km

0	1	2	3	4	5	6	7	8

a. Who heard the thunder first? Why? They all heard it at the same Time. because lightning is so fast ynat in a second it can be heard by all of the people.

b. Who heard it last? Why? They all heard it simoutainesly. because lightning is not ynat well spread out men iny Whos gonna Khow who heard it last.

c. One of the people heard it after about 15 seconds. Who was it? Explain. "S" because "s" cant here something ynat is 15 miles away

d. After how many seconds did the person at *P* hear the thunder? Show how you know. 3 second just Line all of the Rest excpt for "s"

3. Now suppose lightning strikes again at a different place. The person at *P* and the person at *Q* both heard the thunder after the same amount of time.

a. Show on the map below a place where the lightning might have struck.

Right in The center oF P and Q

b. Are there other places where the lightning might have struck? If so, show as many of these places as you can.

c. Can you tell which of *P* and *R* heard the thunder first? If so, say how. If not, say why not.

NO the distance between p and R are too Far apart to be Measured Togetter or at once.

Q ■

P
■

◇   ◇

R
■

◇ ▯

■
S

Scale: 1 cm = 1 km

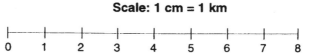

0   1   2   3   4   5   6   7   8

Student A

4. Now suppose lightning strikes once again at yet a different place.
   a. If you know that the person at *P* heard the thunder 9 seconds after she saw the lightning, show on the map as many points as you can where the lightning might have struck.

   b. If you learn that the person at *R* heard the thunder from this same lightning stroke 18 seconds after he saw the lightning, show on the map the places where the lightning might have struck.

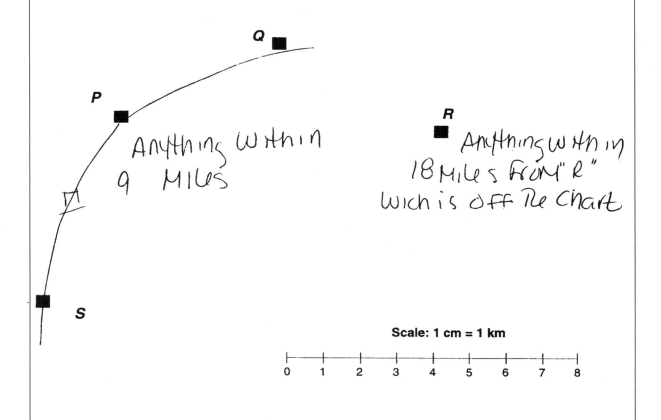

Anything within 9 Miles

Anything within 18 Miles from "R" wich is off the chart

Scale: 1 cm = 1 km

0 1 2 3 4 5 6 7 8

Lightning

This problem gives you the chance to

- *solve problems about real situations involving lightning and thunder*
- *work from a map drawn to scale*
- *use ideas from geometry to reason about distances*

In a thunderstorm, you see the lightning before you hear the thunder.

This is because the light travels essentially instantaneously, whereas the sound of the thunder may take a few seconds to reach you.

One way to estimate the distance from where you are to where the lightning strikes is to count the number of seconds until you hear the thunder, and then divide that number by three. The number you get is the approximate distance in kilometers.

1. Suppose you see a lightning flash, and count 3 seconds before you hear the thunder.
   a. How far away was the lightning? *1 kilometer away*
   b. What does the "divide by three" rule tell you about how fast the sound of thunder travels through the air? Explain.

   It is three seconds different from the lightning

Student B

2. People are standing at the four points *P, Q, R,* and *S* marked in the map below. They all saw lightning strike at point *L.*

Q ■

P
■

R
■

■

L **(lightning)**

■ **S**

Scale: 1 cm = 1 km

```
 ├──┼──┼──┼──┼──┼──┼──┤
 0  1  2  3  4  5  6  7  8
```

a. Who heard the thunder first? Why?

P, it is the closest to L

b. Who heard it last? Why?

R B, it is the farthest away from L.

c. One of the people heard it after about 15 seconds. Who was it? Explain.

d. After how many seconds did the person at *P* hear the thunder? Show how you know.

after 9 seconds

3. Now suppose lightning strikes again at a different place. The person at *P* and the person at *Q* both heard the thunder after the same amount of time.

   a. Show on the map below a place where the lightning might have struck.

   b. Are there other places where the lightning might have struck? If so, show as many of these places as you can.

   c. Can you tell which of *P* and *R* heard the thunder first? If so, say how. If not, say why not.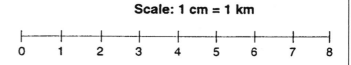

   P, it is closer than R

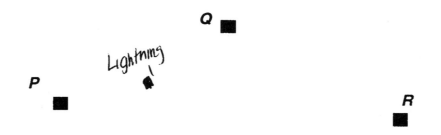

Scale: 1 cm = 1 km

Student B

4. Now suppose lightning strikes once again at yet a different place.
   a. If you know that the person at *P* heard the thunder 9 seconds after she saw the lightning, show on the map as many points as you can where the lightning might have struck.

   b. If you learn that the person at *R* heard the thunder from this same lightning stroke 18 seconds after he saw the lightning, show on the map the places where the lightning might have struck.

Q ■

P
■

R
■

L
◆

■
S

Scale: 1 cm = 1 km

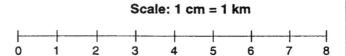

Lightning

This problem gives you the chance to

- *solve problems about real situations involving lightning and thunder*
- *work from a map drawn to scale*
- *use ideas from geometry to reason about distances*

In a thunderstorm, you see the lightning before you hear the thunder.

This is because the light travels essentially instantaneously, whereas the sound of the thunder may take a few seconds to reach you.

One way to estimate the distance from where you are to where the lightning strikes is to count the number of seconds until you hear the thunder, and then divide that number by three. The number you get is the approximate distance in kilometers.

1. Suppose you see a lightning flash, and count 3 seconds before you hear the thunder.
   a. How far away was the lightning?   1 kilometer

   b. What does the "divide by three" rule tell you about how fast the sound of thunder travels through the air? Explain.   It takes three seconds longer to reach a point than the light

2. People are standing at the four points *P, Q, R,* and *S* marked in the map below. They all saw lightning strike at point *L.*

Q ■ 5

P 4.5
■

R
■
5.5

■

L (lightning)

6.5
■ **S**

Scale: 1 cm = 1 km

0   1   2   3   4   5   6   7   8

a. Who heard the thunder first? Why? Ⓠ Because ~~S~~ is The closest one
P   P

b. Who heard it last? Why? Ⓢ Because He is Far away

c. One of the people heard it after about 15 seconds. Who was it? Explain. Q
Q is 5 kilos Away. If you ~~multiply~~ By three
It only Took 15 sec.
multiply

d. After how many seconds did the person at *P* hear the thunder? Show how you know.
4.5 kilos Away Times 3 = 13.5 seconds

Student C

3. Now suppose lightning strikes again at a different place. The person at *P* and the person at *Q* both heard the thunder after the same amount of time.
   a. Show on the map below a place where the lightning might have struck.

   b. Are there other places where the lightning might have struck? If so, show as many of these places as you can.

   c. Can you tell which of *P* and *R* heard the thunder first? If so, say how. If not, say why not. no Because There is no DeFiNaNt Poinras to when it Hit.

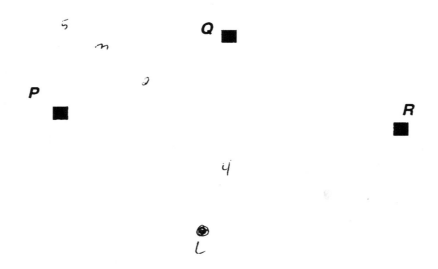

Scale: 1 cm = 1 km

0   1   2   3   4   5   6   7   8

4. Now suppose lightning strikes once again at yet a different place.
   a. If you know that the person at *P* heard the thunder 9 seconds after she saw the lightning, show on the map as many points as you can where the lightning might have struck.

   b. If you learn that the person at *R* heard the thunder from this same lightning stroke 18 seconds after he saw the lightning, show on the map the places where the lightning might have struck.

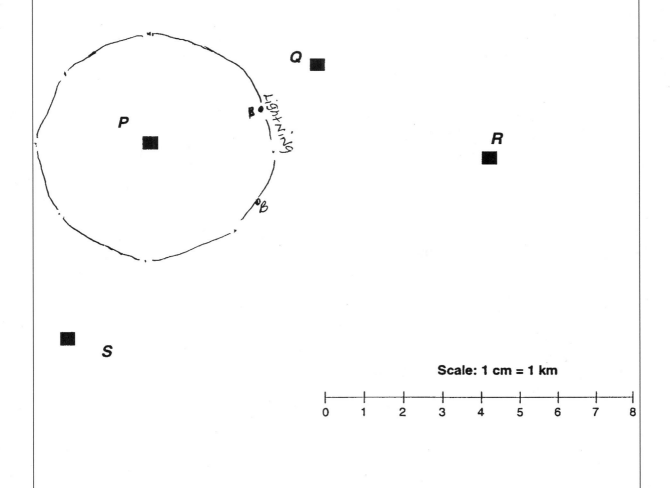

Scale: 1 cm = 1 km

Lightning

This problem gives you the chance to

- *solve problems about real situations involving lightning and thunder*
- *work from a map drawn to scale*
- *use ideas from geometry to reason about distances*

In a thunderstorm, you see the lightning before you hear the thunder.

This is because the light travels essentially instantaneously, whereas the sound of the thunder may take a few seconds to reach you.

One way to estimate the distance from where you are to where the lightning strikes is to count the number of seconds until you hear the thunder, and then divide that number by three. The number you get is the approximate distance in kilometers.

1. Suppose you see a lightning flash, and count 3 seconds before you hear the thunder.
   a. How far away was the lightning?

   1 Kilometer away

   b. What does the "divide by three" rule tell you about how fast the sound of thunder travels through the air? Explain.

   The divide by three rule tells me that it takes the sound of thunder 1 second to go 1/3 of a kilometer in distance if it goes 1 kilometer in three seconds.

2. People are standing at the four points *P, Q, R,* and *S* marked in the map below. They all saw lightning strike at point *L*.

Q ■

P
■

R
■

■

L (lightning)

■
S

Scale: 1 cm = 1 km

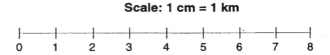

```
|----|----|----|----|----|----|----|----|
0    1    2    3    4    5    6    7    8
```

a. Who heard the thunder first? Why?

P because P is the closest to point L

b. Who heard it last? Why?

S, because S is the furthest away from point L

c. One of the people heard it after about 15 seconds. Who was it? Explain.

Q. Q. heard this after 15 seconds because Q is 5 cm away and if it takes thunder 3 sec per 1 kilometer than that would equal 3 sec x 5 km = 15 s

d. After how many seconds did the person at *P* hear the thunder? Show how you know.

After about 13 or 14 seconds P heard the thunder. I know because if you measure the distance and then multiply by 3 you get the time.

Student D

3. Now suppose lightning strikes again at a different place. The person at *P* and the person at *Q* both heard the thunder after the same amount of time.

   a. Show on the map below a place where the lightning might have struck.

   b. Are there other places where the lightning might have struck? If so, show as many of these places as you can.

   c. Can you tell which of *P* and *R* heard the thunder first? If so, say how. If not, say why not. Yes P heard the thunder first because P is the closest.

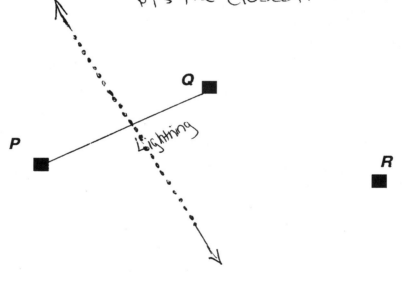

Lightning

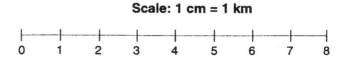

Scale: 1 cm = 1 km

0 1 2 3 4 5 6 7 8

Student D

4. Now suppose lightning strikes once again at yet a different place.
   a. If you know that the person at *P* heard the thunder 9 seconds after she saw the lightning, show on the map as many points as you can where the lightning might have struck. Any where around the circle A

   b. If you learn that the person at *R* heard the thunder from this same lightning stroke 18 seconds after he saw the lightning, show on the map the places where the lightning might have struck.

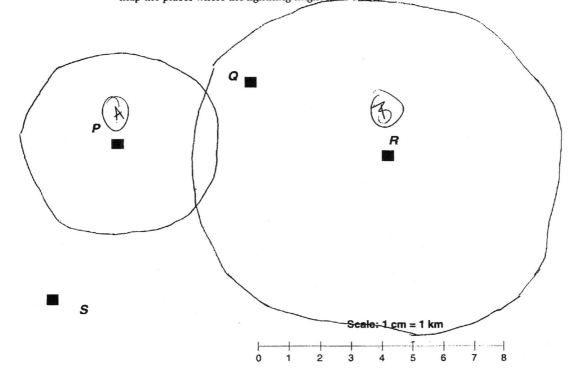

Scale: 1 cm = 1 km

0 1 2 3 4 5 6 7 8

Homework, TV, and Sleep

Analyze the data on
a scatter plot.

Create a scatter plot that
shows positive correlation.

Create a scatter plot that
shows no correlation.

Describe a scatter plot
that shows a negative
correlation.

Short Task

Task Description

This task asks students to analyze the data on a scatter plot by choosing specific points that relate to a given statement and to create a scatter plot that represents two given situations.

The goal is to create a scatter plot for a situation that has a relationship between the two quantities and one for a situation that does not have a relationship between the given quantities.

Assumed Mathematical Background

Students need to have done work with data analysis of graphs, including graphs that show positive correlation and graphs that indicate no correlation between the given quantities.

Core Elements of Performance

- interpret the meaning of the points on a scatter plot
- understand the meaning of a graph that shows a negative correlation
- draw scatter plots to model situations that have positive and zero correlations

Circumstances

Grouping:	Students complete an individual written response.
Materials:	calculator
Estimated time:	15 minutes

Homework, TV, and Sleep

This problem gives you the chance to

- *analyze data on a scatter plot*
- *investigate positive, negative, and zero correlation*

Annie asked a group of teenagers how much time they spent doing homework one evening and how much time they spent watching TV.

Here is a scatter plot to show the results:

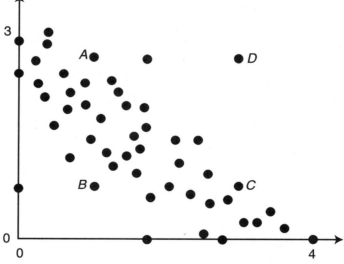

Number of hours spent doing homework

Number of hours spent watching TV

1. Which of the four points *A*, *B*, *C*, or *D* represents each of the statements shown below? Write one letter next to each statement.

I watched a lot of TV last night and I also did a lot of homework.

This is represented by point _____

I spent most of my evening doing homework. I only watched one program on TV.

This is represented by point _____

I went out last night. I didn't do much homework or watch much TV.

This is represented by point _____

2. Make up a statement that matches the fourth point.

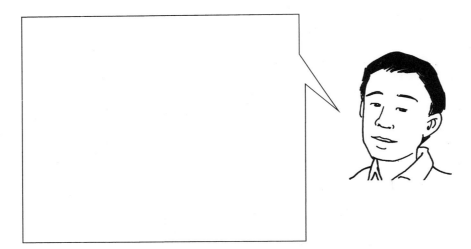

3. What does the graph tell you about the relationship between time spent watching TV and time spent doing homework?

4. Annie also drew scatter plots that showed that:

Older students tend to spend more time doing homework than younger students.

There is no relationship between the time students spend watching TV and the time students spend sleeping.

On the axes below, show what Annie's scatter plots may have looked like.

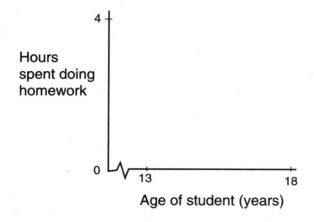

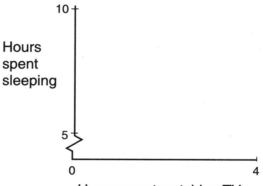

A Sample Solution

1. The points corresponding to the statements are: *D, A, B* respectively.

2. The remaining point, *C*, should be illustrated by a statement such as: "I watched quite a lot of TV but did very little homework."

3. The graph shows a negative correlation between time spent watching TV and time spent doing homework. This means that those who spend more time in front of the TV tend to spend less time doing homework.

4. The scatter plots should look similar to these:

Positive correlation   **No correlation**

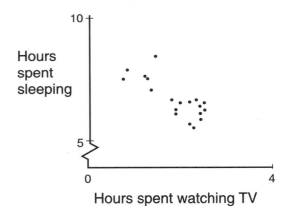

Task

9

Characterizing Performance

This section offers a characterization of student responses and provides indications of the ways in which the students were successful or unsuccessful in engaging with and completing the task. The descriptions are keyed to the *Core Elements of Performance.* Our global descriptions of student work range from "The student needs significant instruction" to "The student's work meets the essential demands of the task." Samples of student work that exemplify these descriptions of performance are included below, accompanied by commentary on central aspects of each student's response. These sample responses are *representative;* they may not mirror the global description of performance in all respects, being weaker in some and stronger in others.

The characterization of student responses for this task is based on these *Core Elements of Performance:*

1. Interpret the meaning of the points on a scatter plot.
2. Understand the meaning of a graph that shows a negative correlation.
3. Draw a scatter plot to model situations that have positive and zero correlations.

Descriptions of Student Work

The student needs significant instruction.

These papers show at most evidence of some understanding of what is required, but the student is not able to interpret the positions of points on the coordinate plane.

Student A

This student had the correct answer for question 1, but then inappropriately changed the second prompt from the correct answer, A, to an incorrect response of C. The student then writes a statement for question 2 that describes the correct point, but that does not correlate with his choices for question 1. His answer to question 3 shows an inability to interpret the scatter plot showing a negative correlation.

The student needs some instruction.

These responses show students that are able to identify the points that correspond to the statements in questions 1 and 2, but they are not able to interpret or display statistical correlations on the scatter plots. Thus, these students might attempt to create a scatter plot for question 4, but it will most likely be incorrect.

Student B

This student gives the correct points in question 1. Her response to question 2 assumes that the student chose to watch TV because his homework did not take too long. She continues this thought in her answer to question 3, because she states that "people on average spend more time watching TV than doing their homework." This response does not allow for a correlation as it does not relate the two variables. She speaks of them as two independent occurrences that have no bearing on each other. Her answer to question 4 does not show a strong enough relationship between the age of a student and the time spent doing homework.

The student's work needs to be revised.

Typically these students can complete the first three questions successfully. They have only limited success in trying to represent situations with positive or zero correlations by means of a scatter plot.

Student C

This student answers questions 1–3 with accuracy. The student's response to question 4 shows the positive and negative correlations, but rather than creating a scatter plot (as indicated in the directions), the student drew a line graph.

The student's work meets the essential demands of the task.

These students are able to interpret scatter plots on a point-by-point basis and can also interpret and sketch scatter plots to represent negative, positive, or zero correlations. Thus they successfully complete all parts of the task.

Student D

This student's response is clear and concise and it meets all of the elements of performance. The student clearly understands the correlations as defined in the task.

Student A

1. Which of the four points *A, B, C,* or *D* represents each of the statements shown below? Write one letter next to each statement.

I watched a lot of TV last night and I also did a lot of homework.

This is represented by point ____D____

I spent most of my evening doing homework. I only watched one program on TV.

This is represented by point ____C____

I went out last night. I didn't do much homework or watch much TV.

This is represented by point ____B____

2. Make up a statement that matches the fourth point.

I spent las night doing a little homework and watching a lot of TV.

3. What does the graph tell you about the relationship between time spent watching TV and time spent doing homework?

most kids spend about the same amount of time watching TV and doing home work

Student B

1. Which of the four points *A, B, C,* or *D* represents each of the statements shown below? Write one letter next to each statement.

| I watched a lot of TV last night and I also did a lot of homework. |

This is represented by point ___D___

| I spent most of my evening doing homework. I only watched one program on TV. |

This is represented by point ___A___

| I went out last night. I didn't do much homework or watch much TV. |

This is represented by point ___B___

2. Make up a statement that matches the fourth point.

> I spent most of my time watching TV but it didn't take me too long To do my Homework

3. What does the graph tell you about the relationship between time spent watching TV and time spent doing homework?

the graph tells me that people on average spend more time watching TV than doing their Homework. And some People have time for both.

4. Annie also drew scatter plots that showed that :_____

Older students tend to spend more time doing homework than younger students.

There is no relationship between the time students spend watching TV and the time students spend sleeping.

On the axes below, show what Annie's scatter plots may have looked like.

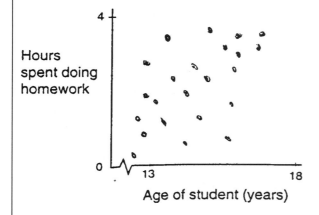

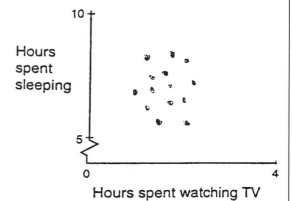

1. Which of the four points *A, B, C,* or *D* represents each of the statements shown below? Write one letter next to each statement.

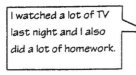

I watched a lot of TV last night and I also did a lot of homework.

This is represented by point ___D___

I spent most of my evening doing homework. I only watched one program on TV.

This is represented by point ___A___

I went out last night. I didn't do much homework or watch much TV.

This is represented by point ___B___

2. Make up a statement that matches the fourth point.

Last night I watched a lot of Television, and I didn't get a lot of homework done.

3. What does the graph tell you about the relationship between time spent watching TV and time spent doing homework?

On an average, the more T.V. watched, The less homework finished and vise versa.

Student C

4. Annie also drew scatter plots that showed that :_____

Older students tend to spend more time doing homework than younger students.

There is no relationship between the time students spend watching TV and the time students spend sleeping.

On the axes below, show what Annie's scatter plots may have looked like.

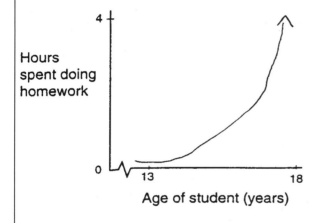

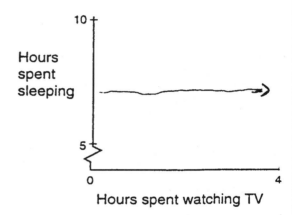

Student D

1. Which of the four points *A*, *B*, *C*, or *D* represents each of the statements shown below? Write one letter next to each statement.

I watched a lot of TV last night and I also did a lot of homework.

This is represented by point ___D___

I spent most of my evening doing homework. I only watched one program on TV.

This is represented by point ___A___

I went out last night. I didn't do much homework or watch much TV.

This is represented by point ___B___

2. Make up a statement that matches the fourth point.

I watched about 3 hours of TV last night and I only Spent 1 hour doing my homework.

- This statement matches Point C.

3. What does the graph tell you about the relationship between time spent watching TV and time spent doing homework?

There is a negative Correlation between time spent watching TV and time spent doing homework. This Graph shows that when people spend less time watching TV they spent more time doing homework, and when they spend more time on homework they spend less watching TV.

4. Annie also drew scatter plots that showed that :_____

Older students tend to spend more time doing homework than younger students.

There is no relationship between the time students spend watching TV and the time students spend sleeping.

On the axes below, show what Annie's scatter plots may have looked like.

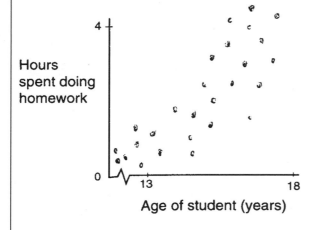

Age of student (years)

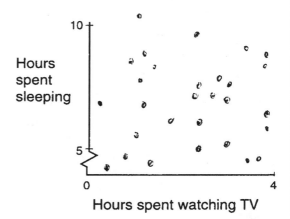

Hours spent watching TV

Wooden Water Tanks

Short Task

Task Description

The components of a large wooden water tank are presented; students are given the number and dimensions of the large wooden slats that are used to make the tank. Students are asked to find the volume of the tank.

Assumed Mathematical Background

It is assumed that students will have experience finding the volume of regular and irregular figures.

Core Elements of Performance

- extract relevant data in a practical situation
- handle units correctly
- apply correct volume formula
- make correct substitutions
- calculate results

Circumstances

Grouping:	Students complete an individual written response.
Materials:	calculator and ruler
Estimated time:	15 minutes

Wooden Water Tanks

This problem gives you the chance to

- *use what you know about volume*
- *model an everyday object using geometry*

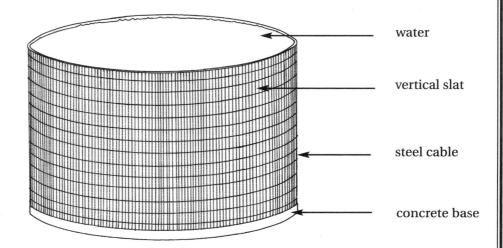

water

vertical slat

steel cable

concrete base

Here is a picture of a large wooden water tank. All measurements are made from the outside of the tank.

The tank is made from 193 vertical slats; each is 5.6 meters long.

The width of each vertical slat is 13.2 cm.

Each vertical slat is 6.3 cm thick.

The base of the tank is made from concrete and is 30 cm thick.

13 steel cables are strapped around the tank.

Each cable is 25.48 meters long.

How much water will one of these tanks hold? Describe your method clearly.

State any decisions that you need to make. State any formula that you use.

A Sample Solution

How much water will the tank hold?
One way to think of this is as the area of a base that is covered in water × height.

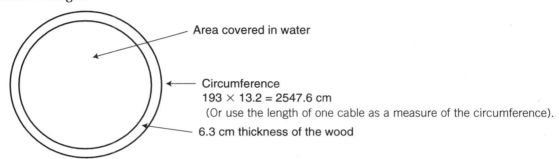

Area covered in water

Circumference
193 × 13.2 = 2547.6 cm
(Or use the length of one cable as a measure of the circumference).

6.3 cm thickness of the wood

Circumference = 193 × 13.2 cm

radius = $\dfrac{193 \times 13.2 \text{ cm}}{2\pi}$ = 405.5 cm

radius of area covered by water = 405.5 cm – 6.3 cm (thickness of wood) = 399.2 cm

area of concrete base that is in contact with water = πr^2 = 500,553.75 cm^2
= 50.0554 m^2

Volume = area × height = 50.0554 m^2 × 5.6 m ≈ 280 m^3

*Note: if rounded value of 399.2 and π = 3.14159 are used, area will be
calculated as 500,645.79 cm^2.

Task

Characterizing Performance

This section offers a characterization of student responses and provides indications of the ways in which the students were successful or unsuccessful in engaging with and completing the task. The descriptions are keyed to the *Core Elements of Performance*. Our global descriptions of student work range from "The student needs significant instruction" to "The student's work meets the essential demands of the task." Samples of student work that exemplify these descriptions of performance are included below, accompanied by commentary on central aspects of each student's response. These sample responses are *representative;* they may not mirror the global description of performance in all respects, being weaker in some and stronger in others.

The characterization of student responses for this task is based on these *Core Elements of Performance:*

1. Extract relevant data in a practical situation.
2. Handle units correctly.
3. Apply correct volume formula.
4. Make correct substitutions.
5. Calculate results.

Descriptions of Student Work

The student needs significant instruction.

These papers show, at most, fragments of work not built into a solution.

Student A

This response annotates the diagram with some incorrect figures, without indicating their derivation, and restates some of the data.

The student needs some instruction.

These papers make some progress by calculating some relevant dimensions, but do not use them in a correct volume formula. There also may be mistakes in converting between meters and centimeters.

Student B

This response obtains a correct value in meters for the external radius (though the calculation is not shown); it then appears to calculate the volume of the wood, and states this as the required volume of water. The units here are wrong. Correct volume formulas are stated, but not used.

The student's work needs to be revised.

These papers show substantially correct methods and results, but with some relatively minor gaps or errors.

Student C

This response obtains a correct expression for the external volume of the tank, though the result of the calculation is illegible. There is also an expression for the volume of the wood (which needs to be subtracted), but this contains an error of unit conversion. This is not evaluated.

The student's work meets the essential demands of the task.

These papers show an essentially correct and complete solution, including all the elements in the sample solution, though not necessarily in the same order. (Note also that there are two alternative ways of obtaining radii.)

Student D

This response is essentially similar to the sample, but uses the more direct way of obtaining the external radius, from the length of the cables.

Wooden Water Tanks

This problem gives you the chance to

■ *use what you know about volume*
■ *model an everyday object using geometry*

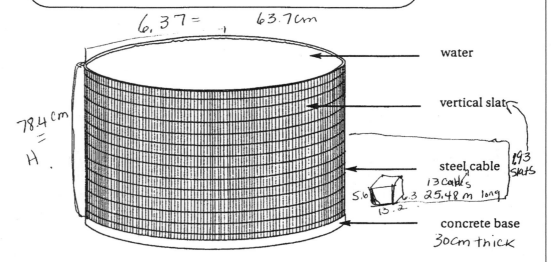

6.37 = 63.7cm

water

vertical slat

78.4 cm = H.

steel cable

193 slats

13 cables

25.48 m long

5.6   6.3

13.2

concrete base
30cm thick

Here is a picture of a large wooden water tank. All measurements are made from the outside of the tank.

The tank is made from 193 vertical slats; each is 5.6 meters long.

The width of each vertical slat is 13.2 cm.

Each vertical slat is 6.3 cm thick.

The base of the tank is made from concrete and is 30 cm thick.

13 steel cables are strapped around the tank.

Each cable is 25.48 meters long.

How much water will one of these tanks hold? Describe your method clearly.

State any decisions that you need to make. State any formula that you use.

Student B

Wooden Water Tanks

This problem gives you the chance to

■ *use what you know about volume*
■ *model an everyday object using geometry*

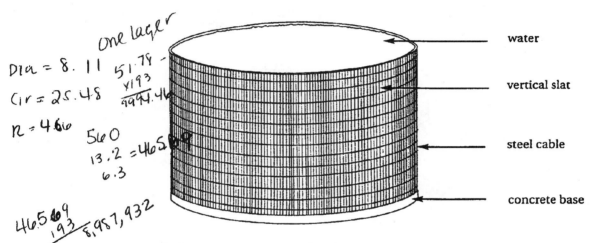

one layer

$Dia = 8.11$ 51.78
$Cir = 25.48$ $\times 193$
                 9994.46

$r = 4.06$

560
$13.2 = 4652.04$
6.3

4652.04
$\times 193$ $8,957,932$

Here is a picture of a large wooden water tank. All measurements are made from the outside of the tank.

$560 cm$

The tank is made from 193 vertical slats; each is 5.6 meters long.

The width of each vertical slat is 13.2 cm.

Each vertical slat is 6.3 cm thick.

The base of the tank is made from concrete and is 30 cm thick.

13 steel cables are strapped around the tank.

2548
Each cable is 25.48 meters long.

How much water will one of these tanks hold? Describe your method clearly.
$89,779,38 m^3$
State any decisions that you need to make. State any formula that you use.

$A = \pi \cdot R^2$ Area of base * height

Wooden Water Tanks

This problem gives you the chance to

■ *use what you know about volume*

■ *model an everyday object using geometry*

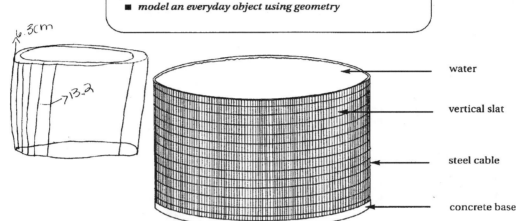

	water
	vertical slat
	steel cable
	concrete base

Here is a picture of a large wooden water tank. All measurements are made from the outside of the tank.

The tank is made from 193 vertical slats; each is 5.60 meters long.

The width of each vertical slat is 13.2 cm.

Each vertical slat is 6.3 cm thick.

The base of the tank is made from concrete and is 30 cm thick.

13 steel cables are strapped around the tank.

Each cable is 25.48 meters long.

How much water will one of these tanks hold? Describe your method clearly.

State any decisions that you need to make. State any formula that you use.

I use the formula $\pi \cdot p^2 \cdot h$. The steel cables are like circumference so you reverse that with the equation circumference π to find the diameter. I got 8.11 rounded to the nearest hundreth that divided by 2 is 4.0 to the nearest hundreth. So we take $\pi \cdot 4.06^2 \cdot 5.6 = 290$ the nearest hundreth. But since the slats have thickness, you have to deduct that thickness from the total 156 meters 6600 cm (13.2 · 6.3)

Wooden Water Tanks

This problem gives you the chance to

- *use what you know about volume*
- *model an everyday object using geometry*

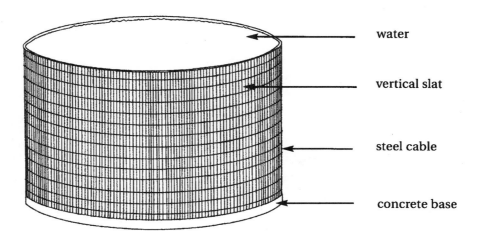

water

vertical slat

steel cable

concrete base

Here is a picture of a large wooden water tank. All measurements are made from the outside of the tank.

The tank is made from 193 vertical slats; each is 5.6 meters long.

The width of each vertical slat is 13.2 cm.

Each vertical slat is 6.3 cm thick.

The base of the tank is made from concrete and is 30 cm thick.

13 steel cables are strapped around the tank.

Each cable is 25.48 meters long.

How much water will one of these tanks hold? Describe your method clearly.

State any decisions that you need to make. State any formula that you use.

Handwritten student work:

Circumference of tank
= 25.48 meters.
So radius is $\frac{25.48}{2\pi}$

= 4.057 m.
This is the external radius
internal = 4.057 - 6.3 cm
= 63
$\frac{}{3.994 m}$

So vol. = $\pi r^2 h$
= 3.14 × 3.994² × 5.6
= 280.5 cu.m.

Task 11

Overview

Read and understand a table.

Use percentages.

Be able to identify inconsistencies.

Where's the Misprint?

Short Task

Task Description

This task shows students a short table from a newspaper that gives the results of an election. But the table has a misprint in it.

Students are asked to show how they could tell there is a misprint without being told there is one. They are then given further information and asked to use it to identify and correct the misprints.

Assumed Mathematical Background

All high school students should be able to tackle this task. It involves only a general understanding of percentages.

Core Elements of Performance

- relate real data and percents
- note inconsistencies
- make trial corrections
- give full numerical explanations
- consider all possibilities

Circumstances

Grouping:	Students complete an individual written response.
Materials:	calculator
Estimated time:	15 minutes

Where's the Misprint?

This problem gives you the chance to

- *read and understand a table*
- *use simple percentages*
- *explain inconsistencies*

The following table appeared in a newspaper following an election:

Measure F

Yes votes	13,657	42%
No votes	186,491	58%

1. If you study this table, you should see that there must have been a misprint. Write a short note to the editor saying how you know that there was a misprint.

2. Suppose you learn that the misprint was of just one digit in the number 13,657. What should that number be and why?

3. Suppose you learn that the misprint was of just one digit in the number 186,491. What should that number be and why?

4. Suppose you learn that the number of yes votes and no votes were correct in the table. How must the rest of the table be changed?

A Sample Solution

	Measure F	
Yes votes	13,657	42%
No votes	186,491	58%

1. To the editor:
   There is something wrong with the numbers in the table for Measure F in the newspaper. The number of no votes (186,491) is more than ten times the number of yes votes (13,657), but the no-vote percentage (58%) is not nearly ten times the yes-vote percentage (42%). So either the numbers or the percentages must be off. What are the correct figures?

2. If the misprint was only in the number 13,657, then that number needs to be larger. It is reasonable to think that a digit was left off the end by mistake. Let's try 136,570. Then the total votes are 136,570 + 186,491 = 323,061. Now 136,570 ÷ 323,061 ≈ 0.423 ≈ 42%. So, if 13,657 was 136,570, the table would be consistent.

3. If the misprint was only in the number 186,491, then that number needs to be smaller. Let's try dropping the last digit to give 18,649. Then the total votes are 13,657 + 18,649 = 32,306. Now 18,649 ÷ 32,306 ≈ 0.577 ≈ 58%. So, if 186,491 was 18,649, the table would be consistent.

4. If the number of yes votes and no votes are correct in the table, then we can compute the correct percentages. First, the total votes are 13,657 + 186,491 = 200,148. Now, dividing gives 13,657 ÷ 200,148 ≈ 0.068 ≈ 7%. So the yes percentage would be about 7%, and the no percentage about 93%.

Task

Characterizing Performance

This section offers a characterization of student responses and provides indications of the ways in which the students were successful or unsuccessful in engaging with and completing the task. The descriptions are keyed to the *Core Elements of Performance*. Our global descriptions of student work range from "The student needs significant instruction" to "The student's work meets the essential demands of the task." Samples of student work that exemplify these descriptions of performance are included below, accompanied by commentary on central aspects of each student's response. These sample responses are *representative;* they may not mirror the global description of performance in all respects, being weaker in some and stronger in others.

The characterization of student responses for this task is based on these *Core Elements of Performance:*

1. Relate real data and percents.
2. Note inconsistencies.
3. Make trial corrections.
4. Give full numerical explanations.
5. Consider all possibilities.

Descriptions of Student Work

The student needs significant instruction.

These papers show at most an understanding that digits must be changed to meet given constraints, but without any apparent idea of how this might be done.

Student A

This response suggests some possible changes, but there is no understanding of the nature of the constraints, nor of the correctness of the percents adding to 100.

The student needs some instruction.

These papers show an understanding of the nature of the task, but the students are apparently unable to check their suggestions numerically and so they do not provide justifications for them.

Student B

This response shows some weak suggestions, one of which is correct, but no check or justification is offered.

The student's work needs to be revised.

These papers show an appropriate strategy for the task, and substantially correct results, with possibly some relatively minor gaps or errors.

Student C

This response shows sensible approaches to all questions, but the answers to half of them are incorrect. However, it is clear from the correct numerical response to the last question that the student has the necessary competence to make calculations using percent.

The student's work meets the essential demands of the task.

These papers show essentially fully correct answers and justifications.

Student D

This response is fully correct, and also shows awareness that there is not just one correct answer in 2 and 3, but several possibilities. The very full response goes beyond what one might reasonably expect.

Student A

Where's the Misprint?

This problem gives you the chance to

- *read and understand a table*
- *use simple percentages*
- *explain inconsistencies*

The following table appeared in a newspaper following an election:

	Measure F	
Yes votes	13,657	42%
No votes	186,491	58%

1. If you study this table, you should see that there must have been a misprint. Write a short note to the editor saying how you know that there was a misprint.

   If you add up the two numbers it equals 200,148 and it should be a whole number because the percents equal 100%.

2. Suppose you learn that the misprint was of just one digit in the number 13,657. What should that number be and why?

   It should be the 7 that changes to a 9 because then it would make it a whole number.

3. Suppose you learn that the misprint was of just one digit in the number 186,491. What should that number be and why?

   It should be the 1 changed to a 3 because the numbers have to be an even amount.

4. Suppose you learn that the number of yes votes and no votes were correct in the table. How must the rest of the table be changed?

   The percents should be different and shouldn't add up to 100%

Where's the Misprint?

This problem gives you the chance to

- *read and understand a table*
- *use simple percentages*
- *explain inconsistencies*

The following table appeared in a newspaper following an election:

Measure F		
Yes votes	13,657	42%
No votes	186,491	58%

1. If you study this table, you should see that there must have been a misprint. Write a short note to the editor saying how you know that there was a misprint. The misprint is in the number of votes that there was.

2. Suppose you learn that the misprint was of just one digit in the number 13,657. What should that number be and why? The number should be 8.

3. Suppose you learn that the misprint was of just one digit in the number 186,491. What should that number be and why? The number would be 8 because you need to take the 9 out to make the percentages right.

4. Suppose you learn that the number of yes votes and no votes were correct in the table. How must the rest of the table be changed? The percentage of no votes needs to be increased and the yes votes needs to decrease.

Student C

Where's the Misprint?

This problem gives you the chance to

- *read and understand a table*
- *use simple percentages*
- *explain inconsistencies*

The following table appeared in a newspaper following an election:

Measure F

Yes votes	13,657	42%
No votes	186,491	58%

total = 200,148

1. If you study this table, you should see that there must have been a misprint. Write a short note to the editor saying how you know that there was a misprint.

   THe Percentes are not Contrasting enough FoR the Data

2. Suppose you learn that the misprint was of just one digit in the number 13,657. What should that number be and why? 13,675 = 93,675 to have less of a Contrast between yes and no

3. Suppose you learn that the misprint was of just one digit in the number 186,491. What should that number be and why? 186,491 = 106,491 to have less of a Contrast between yes and no

4. Suppose you learn that the number of yes votes and no votes were correct in the table. How must the rest of the table be changed? The % has to be Changed to yes = 7%   no = 93%

Where's the Misprint?

This problem gives you the chance to

- *read and understand a table*
- *use simple percentages*
- *explain inconsistencies*

The following table appeared in a newspaper following an election:

Measure F

Yes votes	13,657	42%
No votes	186,491	58%

1. If you study this table, you should see that there must have been a misprint.
   Write a short note to the editor saying how you know that there was a misprint.

   Dear editor, The percents on measure F are close but the number are way off. There must be a misprint.

2. Suppose you learn that the misprint was of just one digit in the number 13,657. What should that number be and why?

   There could be a figure missing after the 3: 0 Gives 130657/317418 = 41%. 9 Gives 139657/186491 = 44%. But anything between 3 (41.7%) and 7 (42.4%) works

3. Suppose you learn that the misprint was of just one digit in the number 186,491. What should that number be and why?

   There is a digit too many. It might be the final 1: 13657/32306 = 423] But as in no. 3 there are other possibilities.

4. Suppose you learn that the number of yes votes and no votes were correct in the table. How must the rest of the table be changed?

   The %'s should be 7% and 93%

12

The Knockout

Short Task

Task Description

Three tennis players compare the number of wins and losses each has had. Students are asked to use this information to figure out the probability of each player's winning the upcoming game.

Assumed Mathematical Background

All high school students are likely to be able to tackle this task with a high degree of success. It is essential that the student has encountered concepts of probability.

Core Elements of Performance

- consider all possible outcomes of a situation
- calculate simple probabilities
- calculate probabilities of combined events given the probability of independent events

Circumstances

Grouping:	Students complete an individual written response.
Materials:	calculator
Estimated time:	15 minutes

The Knockout

This problem gives you the chance to

- *figure out the probability of each person's winning a game of tennis*

Rani, Tony, and Sarah have entered a tennis knockout competition.
They have played each other before.

Rani

So far against Tony, I have won 12 matches and lost 8 matches.

Tony

So far against Sarah, I have won 10 matches and lost 20 matches.

Sarah

I have won a third of the matches I have played against Rani.

In the tournament, Rani will play Tony.
The winner will then play Sarah.

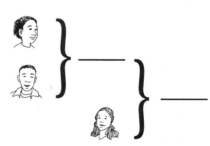

What is the probability of each person's winning the tournament?

Show your reasoning and calculations as clearly as you can.

A Sample Solution

The tree diagram below shows the possible outcomes and estimates of their probabilities.

First match   **Second Match**

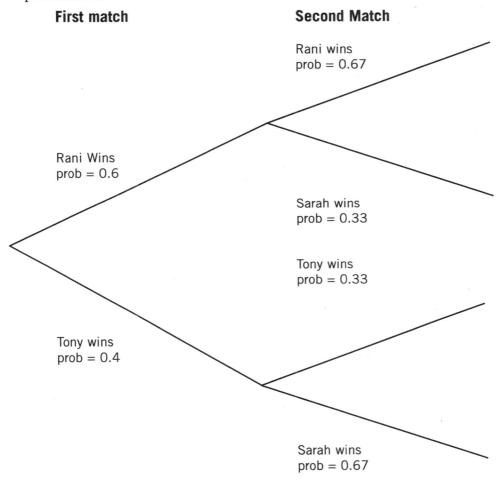

Rani wins
prob = 0.67

Rani Wins
prob = 0.6

Sarah wins
prob = 0.33

Tony wins
prob = 0.33

Tony wins
prob = 0.4

Sarah wins
prob = 0.67

Thus the probability that Rani wins is $0.6 \times 0.67 = 0.4$ (or $\frac{6}{15}$)

The probability that Sarah wins is $(0.6 \times 0.33) + (0.4 \times 0.67) = 0.47$ (or $\frac{7}{15}$)

The probability that Tony wins is $0.4 \times 0.33 = 0.13$ (or $\frac{2}{15}$)

So, Sarah is marginally the most likely to win.

Task

12

Characterizing Performance

This section offers a characterization of student responses and provides indications of the ways in which the students were successful or unsuccessful in engaging with and completing the task. The descriptions are keyed to the *Core Elements of Performance*. Our global descriptions of student work range from "The student needs significant instruction" to "The student's work meets the essential demands of the task." Samples of student work that exemplify these descriptions of performance are included below, accompanied by commentary on central aspects of each student's response. These sample responses are *representative;* they may not mirror the global description of performance in all respects, being weaker in some and stronger in others.

The characterization of student responses for this task is based on these *Core Elements of Performance:*

1. Consider all possible outcomes of a situation.
2. Calculate simple probabilities.
3. Calculate probabilities of combined events given the probability of independent events.

Descriptions of Student Work

The student needs significant instruction.

These papers show at most evidence that the student has understood the requirements of the task. These papers lack calculations and reasoning is often incorrect.

Student A

This student has shown that he understands the nature of a knockout tournament and has calculated some ratios based on the data. The student, however, does not show any reasoning or calculations, and incorrectly states that Rani will win.

The student needs some instruction.

The student has understood the requirements of the task and has made some attempt to translate the given data into probabilities. The student does not, however, show an understanding of how these probabilities may be used to calculate the probability of a combined event. Reasoning is unclear and incomplete.

Student B

This response shows that the student has calculated the probability that Rani will beat Tony $\left(\frac{12}{20}\right)$ and that Tony will beat Rani $\left(\frac{8}{20}\right)$. This student does not know what to do with these probabilities and resorts to reasoning based solely on the number of matches to be played.

The student's work needs to be revised.

The student has calculated a probability for each of the possible outcomes using an appropriate method. The student has attempted to combine the probabilities, but the solution contains significant gaps or errors. The student may, for example, have attempted to use a tree diagram or to combine correct probabilities, but has forgotten to take into account all possible outcomes. The reasoning is mostly clear and easy to follow.

Student C

This student's calculated probabilities are mostly correct. The probability of Sarah's winning, however, is incorrect. Student C did not add probabilities to check for a 1 sum, so the mistake was not caught.

The student's work meets the essential demands of the task.

The student has calculated a probability for each of the possible outcomes using an appropriate method. The student recognizes when it is appropriate to add and multiply probabilities. The student has shown clear reasoning and the working is easy to follow. The solution is correct, apart from at most a minor slip in calculation.

Student D

This student has produced a clear account of the method, showing the calculations for the probabilities of wins by Rani and by Tony and thus deduces the probability of Sarah's winning.

Student A

The Knockout

This problem gives you the chance to

- *figure out the probability of each person's winning a game of tennis*

Rani, Tony, and Sarah have entered a tennis knockout competition. They have played each other before.

Rani   **Tony**   **Sarah**

$3:2 \rightarrow$ $1:3$ ↘ $1:3$

> So far against Tony, I have won 12 matches and lost 8 matches.

> So far against Sarah, I have won 10 matches and lost 20 matches.

> I have won a third of the matches I have played against Rani.

In the tournament, Rani will play Tony. The winner will then play Sarah.

} Rani } Rani

What is the probability of each person's winning the tournament?

Show your reasoning and calculations as clearly as you can.

Rani will win

The Knockout

This problem gives you the chance to

■ *figure out the probability of each person's winning a game of tennis*

Rani, Tony, and Sarah have entered a tennis knockout competition. They have played each other before.

Rani

So far against Tony, I have won 12 matches and lost 8 matches.

Tony

So far against Sarah, I have won 10 matches and lost 20 matches.

Sarah

I have won a third of the matches I have played against Rani.

In the tournament, Rani will play Tony. The winner will then play Sarah.

$R = \frac{12}{20}$
$T = \frac{8}{20}$

What is the probability of each person's winning the tournament?

Show your reasoning and calculations as clearly as you can.

Sarah has a much better chance because she only has to win one match, where Tony and Rani have to win 2.

The Knockout

This problem gives you the chance to

- *figure out the probability of each person's winning a game of tennis*

Rani, Tony, and Sarah have entered a tennis knockout competition. They have played each other before.

Rani

Tony

Sarah

So far against Tony, I have won 12 matches and lost 8 matches.

So far against Sarah, I have won 10 matches and lost 20 matches.

I have won a third of the matches I have played against Rani.

In the tournament, Rani will play Tony. The winner will then play Sarah.

Tony 2|5
Rani 3|5

Tony 2|5 2%
Sarah 1/3 33%
Rani 2/5 40%

What is the probability of each person's winning the tournament?

Show your reasoning and calculations as clearly as you can.

Tony 2|5 (2/5 x 1/3)

Sarah 1/3

Rani 2|5 (3/5 x 2/3)

Student D

The Knockout

This problem gives you the chance to

■ *figure out the probability of each person's winning a game of tennis*

Rani, Tony, and Sarah have entered a tennis knockout competition.
They have played each other before.

Rani   **Tony**   **Sarah**

So far against Tony, I have won 12 matches and lost 8 matches.

So far against Sarah, I have won 10 matches and lost 20 matches.

I have won a third of the matches I have played against Rani.

60% W
40% LVT

33.3% U
66.6%

33.3% W
66.6% L

In the tournament, Rani will play Tony.
The winner will then play Sarah.

R=60%
T=40%

R→66.6% R 533.3%
T→33.3% T 66.1% S

What is the probability of each person's winning the tournament?

Show your reasoning and calculations as clearly as you can. Rani has a 60% chance of moving to the second round (12/20) so Tony has a 40% (8/20) chance. Sarah would have a 33.3% chance of winning the tournament if she faced Rani + a 66.6% chance if she faced Tony. Rani would have 1st Percentage 2nd Percentage .6×.66 or 40% chance of winning the whole tournament .6×.66. Tony has a .4×.33% or 13.3% chance of winning the tournament That would leave Sarah a 46.6% chance of winning.

Shadows

Use similar triangles in analyzing shadows.

Construct formulas showing the relation of shadow length to distance from the light.

Short Task

Task Description

Students are given a diagram showing the shadow of a person standing beside a lamppost.

They are asked questions about how the shadow length varies as the person moves around, and as people with different heights are considered.

Assumed Mathematical Background

Students need to have worked with the concept of similar triangles.

Core Elements of Performance

- use ratio to find a fourth length when three are known

- recognize and graph a proportional relationship and represent this using a formula

- recognize how this relationship will change as one of the variables is altered

Circumstances

Grouping:	Students complete an individual written response.
Materials:	calculator
Estimated time:	15 minutes

Shadows

This problem gives you the chance to

- *use a combination of geometry and algebra to solve an applied problem about shadows*

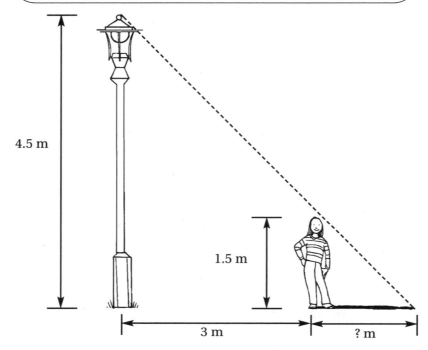

4.5 m

1.5 m

3 m

? m

1. Alice is 1.5 m tall. She is standing 3 m from the foot of a lamppost. The lamp is 4.5 m from the ground. How long will Alice's shadow be?

2. How will the length of Alice's shadow vary as she walks around? Answer this question using a graph. Can you find a formula to fit this graph?

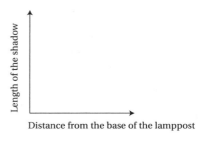

Length of the shadow

Distance from the base of the lamppost

3. Simon is 2 m tall. Suppose you repeated question 2 for Simon. How would his graph compare with the one you drew for Alice? Sketch your ideas and explain your reasoning.

A Sample Solution

1.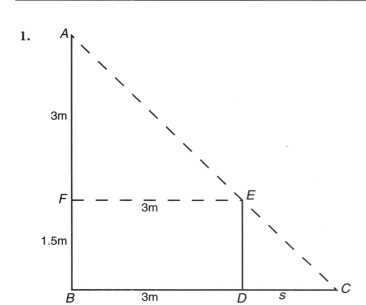

The lamppost is represented by *AB*, and Alice is represented by *ED*.
Her shadow length is given by *s*.
From the diagram we can see that △*AFE* is similar to △*EDC*.
Since △*AFE* is isosceles, so is △*EDC*. This means that $s = 1.5$ m.

2. Let *d* be Alice's distance from the lamppost as she walks around. Then
   $BD = FE = d$. Because similar triangles have corresponding sides that are
   proportional, $\frac{FE}{AF} = \frac{s}{ED}$. Since $AF = 3$ and $ED = 1.5$ (and these values don't
   change), we see that $s = ED\frac{FE}{AF} = (1.5)\frac{d}{3} = \frac{1}{2}d$. So as Alice walks around,
   s varies according to the formula $s = \frac{1}{2}d$. Thus the graph should be a
   straight line through the origin with a slope of $\frac{1}{2}$.

3. The only change for Simon is that his height *ED* is 2 m, so that
   AF becomes 2.5 m. Thus the formula becomes $s = ED\frac{FE}{AF} = (2)\frac{d}{2.5} = \frac{4}{5}d$.
   Hence, *s* will vary according to the formula $s = \frac{4}{5}d$. His graph will thus be
   a straight line with a steeper slope (slope $= \frac{4}{5}$) than Alice's graph.

Characterizing Performance

Task

This section offers a characterization of student responses and provides indications of the ways in which the students were successful or unsuccessful in engaging with and completing the task. The descriptions are keyed to the *Core Elements of Performance*. Our global descriptions of student work range from "The student needs significant instruction" to "The student's work meets the essential demands of the task." Samples of student work that exemplify these descriptions of performance are included below, accompanied by commentary on central aspects of each student's response. These sample responses are *representative;* they may not mirror the global description of performance in all respects, being weaker in some and stronger in others.

The characterization of student responses for this task is based on these *Core Elements of Performance:*

1. Use a ratio to find a fourth length when three are known.
2. Recognize and graph a proportional relationship and represent this using a formula.
3. Recognize how this relationship will change as one of the variables is altered.

Descriptions of Student Work

The student needs significant instruction.

These papers show at most evidence that the student has understood the requirements of the task.

Student A

This student understands the questions and has made an attempt at answering all three parts, but shows no understanding of any appropriate method for question 1. Her responses to questions 2 and 3 show that she appears to have little understanding of the relationship between the variables involved.

The student needs some instruction.

These papers show that the student has understood the requirements of the task, but there is no evidence that the student recognizes an appropriate method for tackling the problem. The student may have some understanding of the nature of the relationship between the variables involved in the problem, but he/she cannot represent this algebraically.

Student B

In this response, the student has inappropriately attempted to use the Pythagorean theorem for question 1 of the problem. This student has some appreciation of the qualitative relationship between the length of the shadow and the distance from the lamppost, but she does not use any calculations to justify her response.

The student's work needs to be revised.

The student recognizes and uses an appropriate method to solve the problem, but the solution may contain significant errors. The student has understood how to represent the dependency of shadow length on the height of the lamppost using a graph. The student has also shown a proportional relationship, though this may not have been represented algebraically. Typically the student has answered questions 1 and 2 quite well.

Student C

This student has attempted to use a ratio method, although an error has been made in the selection of appropriate triangles to use. Thus he has used $\frac{4.5}{1.5} = \frac{3}{x}$ instead of $\frac{4.5}{1.5} = \frac{(3+x)}{x}$. Although this is a serious error, the script goes on to show that the student recognizes that the shadow length is proportional to the distance from the lamppost and has represented his own relationship algebraically. He has also adapted his own result correctly for a taller person; he recognizes that the ratio Simon:Alice is 4:3.

The student's work meets the essential demands of the task.

The student recognizes and successfully uses an appropriate method to solve the problem. The student understands how to represent the dependency of shadow length on the height of the lamppost using a suitable graph and formula, *and* has shown how such a graph may be adapted for a different person's height.

Student D

Student D has answered all questions quite well, though the presentation of the work leaves something to be desired.

Shadows

This problem gives you the chance to

■ *use a combination of geometry and algebra to solve an applied problem about shadows*

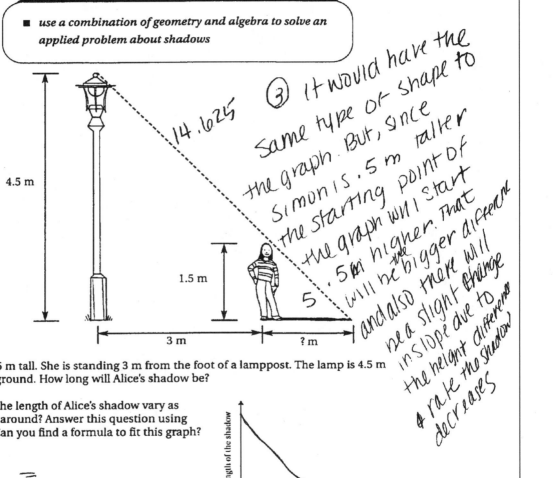

D = Post

4.5 m

1.5 m

3 m   ? m

14.625

③ It would have the same type of shape to the graph. But, since Simon is .5 m taller the starting point of the graph will start 5 .5m higher. That will be bigger difference and also there will be a slight change in slope due to the height difference a rate the shadow decreases

1. Alice is 1.5 m tall. She is standing 3 m from the foot of a lamppost. The lamp is 4.5 m from the ground. How long will Alice's shadow be?

2. How will the length of Alice's shadow vary as she walks around? Answer this question using a graph. Can you find a formula to fit this graph?

$$L =$$

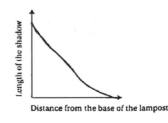

length of the shadow

Distance from the base of the lampost

3. Simon is 2 m tall. Suppose you repeated question 2 for Simon. How would his graph compare with the one you drew for Alice? Sketch your ideas and explain your reasoning.

Student B

Shadows

This problem gives you the chance to

■ *use a combination of geometry and algebra to solve an applied problem about shadows*

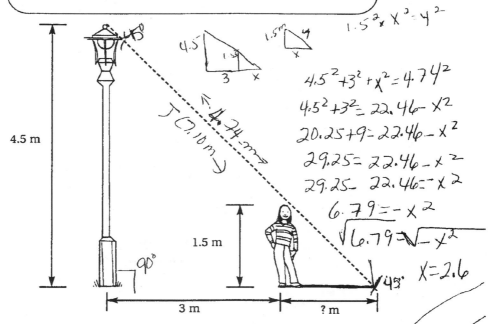

$$1.5^2 + x^2 = y^2$$

$$4.5^2 + 3^2 + x^2 = 4.74^2$$

$$4.5^2 + 3^2 = 22.46 - x^2$$

$$20.25 + 9 = 22.46 - x^2$$

$$29.25 = 22.46 - x^2$$

$$29.25 - 22.46 = x^2$$

$$6.79 = -x^2$$

$$\sqrt{6.79} = \sqrt{-x^2}$$

$$x = 2.6$$

4.5 m

1.5 m

90°

45°

3 m

? m

1. Alice is 1.5 m tall. She is standing 3 m from the foot of a lamppost. The lamp is 4.5 m from the ground. How long will Alice's shadow be?

   ·2.6 m

2. How will the length of Alice's shadow vary as she walks around? Answer this question using a graph. Can you find a formula to fit this graph? AS

   DxIxa She walkes toward the lamp post the shadow will decrease if she walkes away from it, will her shadow length increase.

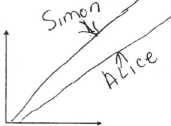

Length of the shadow

Distance from the base of the lampost

Simon

Alice

3. Simon is 2 m tall. Suppose you repeated question 2 for Simon. How would his graph He is taller and he will have an longer shadow compare with the one you drew for Alice? Sketch your ideas and explain your reasoning.

Shadows

This problem gives you the chance to

■ *use a combination of geometry and algebra to solve an applied problem about shadows*

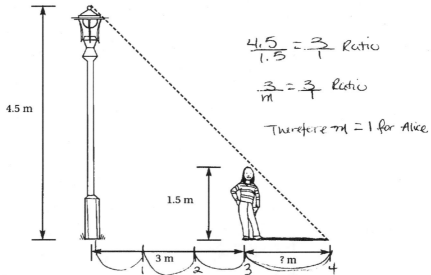

4.5 m

1.5 m

3 m   ? m

$$\frac{4.5}{1.5} = \frac{3}{1} \quad Ratio$$

$$\frac{3}{m} = \frac{3}{1} \quad Ratio$$

Therefore m = 1 for Alice

1. Alice is 1.5 m tall. She is standing 3 m from the foot of a lamppost. The lamp is 4.5 m from the ground. How long will Alice's shadow be?
   Alice's shadow will be 1 meter

2. How will the length of Alice's shadow vary as she walks around? Answer this question using a graph. Can you find a formula to fit this graph?
   y = .33x + 0

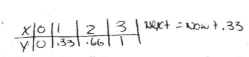

next = now + .33

The slope of Simon's line will be steeper because he was taller than 3. Alice

3. Simon is 2 m tall. Suppose you repeated question 2 for Simon. How would his graph compare with the one you drew for Alice? Sketch your ideas and explain your reasoning. y = .44x + 0 $\frac{4.5}{2} = \frac{2.25}{1}$ Ratio

X	0	1	2	3	4
Y	0	.44	.88	1.33	1.77

Student D

Shadows

This problem gives you the chance to

■ *use a combination of geometry and algebra to solve an applied problem about shadows*

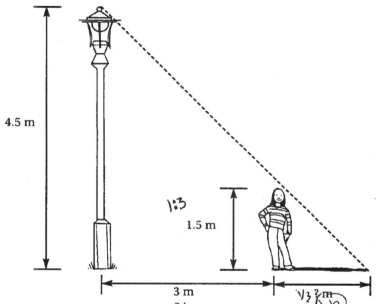

4.5 m

1:3

1.5 m

3 m   ⅓ 2 m

²/₃

⅓ ÷ ⅔ = ½

1. Alice is 1.5 m tall. She is standing 3 m from the foot of a lamppost. The lamp is 4.5 m from the ground. How long will Alice's shadow be? 1.5 meters

the further she is from the lamp the longer her shadow will be

2. How will the length of Alice's shadow vary as she walks around? Answer this question using a graph. Can you find a formula to fit this graph?

$$y = \frac{1}{2}x$$

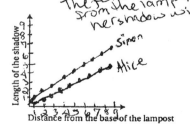

Length of the shadow

Simon

Alice

1 2 3 4 5 6 7 8 9
Distance from the base of the lampost

3. Simon is 2 m tall. Suppose you repeated question 2 for Simon. How would his graph compare with the one you drew for Alice? Sketch your ideas and explain your reasoning. It would be steeper. You must find the ratio of the 2 heights

$4/9 ÷ 5/9 = .8$ or $4/5$

$$y = 4/5x$$

$$\frac{h_2}{h_1} = \frac{2}{4.5} = \frac{4}{9}$$

h_1 h_2 b_1 b_2 $5/9$ $4/9$

Something's Fishy

Use sampling techniques to draw conclusions about a large population.

Use basic ideas of proportional reasoning to interpret a sample.

Short Task

Task Description

A situation is described in which a sample of fish is taken from a lake. In this sample, one type of fish is counted and tagged. These fish are then put back in the lake. A second sample is taken later, and the tagged and untagged fish of the same kind are counted, as well as the total sample size.

Students are then asked to make conclusions about the numbers of different kinds of fish in the lake.

Assumed Mathematical Background

Students should have had some exposure to the idea of taking a sample from a large population. They also need to understand basic proportional reasoning.

Core Elements of Performance

- convert numbers to proportions and percents
- construct a block graph or pie chart
- infer numbers in a population from data for a sample

Circumstances

Grouping:	Students complete an individual written response.
Materials:	calculator
Estimated time:	15 minutes

Something's Fishy

This problem gives you the chance to

- *use the information presented here to try to figure out an estimate of different fish populations*

The California Department of Fish and Game needs statistics on the trout population in a Sierra lake to make decisions about fishing limits. Your team has been sent out to take samples of the fish in the lake.

Dragging a large net behind a boat, you catch a good sample of fish. After counting the sample, your team finds the following counts:

      Brown trout: 70 fish
      Rainbow trout: 42 fish
      Other fish: 56 fish

1. What is your best guess of the proportions of the different fish populations in the lake, based on the sample? Create a chart or graph to show this.

Your team then puts identification tags on each of the trout (both Brown and Rainbow), but not the other fish, and releases all the fish back into the lake.

After allowing the fish to mix with the others in the lake, your team takes another sample with the following results:

Brown trout:
    tagged: 15 fish
    untagged: 61 fish

Rainbow trout:
    tagged: 9 fish
    untagged: 36 fish

Other fish (all untagged): 60 fish

2. Prepare a report that tells the total number of each kind of fish in the lake. Include charts and/or graphs, as appropriate, and explain how the samples helped you find the total populations.

Task

A Sample Solution

14

1. Here is the relevant data presented in a table.

First sample	Brown trout	Rainbow trout	Other fish	Total
numbers	70	42	56	168
proportions	0.42	0.25	0.33	1.00

A histogram with three labeled columns with heights proportional to these quantities would accomplish the task, as would any of several other types of graph.

2. Here is some data about the total numbers (tagged and untagged) caught in the second sample.

Second sample	Brown trout	Rainbow trout	Other fish	Total
numbers	76	45	60	181
proportions	0.42	0.25	0.33	1.00

The interesting thing here is that the same proportions of fish are caught in each of the two samples. This means that the sampling technique seems to give consistent results from one sample to the next.

The next thing to observe is that exactly one fifth (9 out of 45) of the Rainbow trout caught in the second sample were already tagged, and approximately one fifth (15 out of 76) of the Brown trout caught in the second sample were already tagged.

This suggests that the tagged Brown trout in the lake are about one fifth of the total number of Brown trout. We know that 70 are tagged, so there must be about five times this number in all. Similarly for the Rainbow trout. And since we are assuming that the proportions of the different fish are the same in total as in the two samples, the number of other fish must be 5×56. Here is a table:

Total population (assumed)	Brown trout	Rainbow trout	Other fish	Total
numbers	$5 \times 70 = 350$	$5 \times 42 = 210$	$5 \times 56 = 280$	$5 \times 168 = 840$
proportions	0.42	0.25	0.33	1.00

A graph or histogram of this would look very much like the one in question 1.

Characterizing Performance

This section offers a characterization of student responses and provides indications of the ways in which the students were successful or unsuccessful in engaging with and completing the task. The descriptions are keyed to the *Core Elements of Performance.* Our global descriptions of student work range from "The student needs significant instruction" to "The student's work meets the essential demands of the task." Samples of student work that exemplify these descriptions of performance are included below, accompanied by commentary on central aspects of each student's response. These sample responses are *representative;* they may not mirror the global description of performance in all respects, being weaker in some and stronger in others.

The characterization of student responses for this task is based on these *Core Elements of Performance:*

1. Convert numbers to proportions and percents.
2. Construct a block graph or pie chart.
3. Infer numbers in a population from data for a sample.

Descriptions of Student Work

The student needs significant instruction.

These papers show at most some kind of chart of the data given. Typically, proportions are not calculated and there is no response to question 2.

Student A

This response shows an inappropriate point graph of the data, with no estimate of proportions beyond "There are a lot of Brown trout...." There is also no response to question 2.

The student needs some instruction.

These papers calculate proportions and show one or two graphs for question 1. They do not show understanding of the sampling principle in question 2. Typically they treat the second sample as the total.

Task

14

Student B

This response has correct proportion percentages and the student created both a block graph and a pie chart for question 1 to demonstrate the sample. For question 2, the student simply adds the numbers in the second sample.

The student's work needs to be revised.

These papers show correct responses to question 1 and an understanding of the principle of inference from samples in question 2. Typically they comment on the consistency of the proportions in the first and second samples. They calculate totals by using the tagged/untagged ratio. Some gap or calculation error excludes them from the fully correct category.

Student C

This response shows correct percents and a pie chart for question 1. In question 2, the principle of sampling inference is used, but it is incorrect in two respects: 4 times the tagged number actually gives the untagged number, but this is stated as the total; and the numbers in the *second* sample are taken as the number to multiply by 4, whereas it is the numbers in the *first* sample that are known to be the total numbers of each kind tagged.

The student's work meets the essential demands of the task.

These papers show a full understanding of the requirements of the tasks, giving a complete and correct solution.

Student D

This response is fully correct. In question 1, the appropriate percentages and graph for the sample are shown. In question 2, the proportions are calculated, the consistency is noted and commented upon as an assurance of reliability. Inference from the tagged/untagged ratio and the proportions of the different fish are correctly used to give an estimate for the totals. Everything is well explained.

Something's Fishy

This problem gives you the chance to

■ *use the information presented here to try to figure out an estimate of different fish populations*

The California Department of Fish and Game needs statistics on the trout population in a Sierra lake to make decisions about fishing limits. Your team has been sent out to take samples of the fish in the lake.

Dragging a large net behind a boat, you catch a good sample of fish. After counting the sample, your team finds the following counts:

Brown trout: 70 fish
Rainbow trout: 42 fish
Other fish: 56 fish

1. What is your best guess of the proportions of the different fish populations in the lake, based on the sample? Create a chart or graph to show this.

There are alot of Brown trout, a medium population of other types of fish, & not very many rainbow trout.

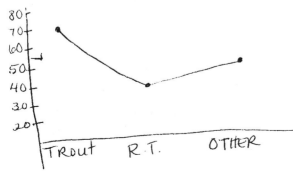

Something's Fishy

This problem gives you the chance to

■ *use the information presented here to try to figure out an estimate of different fish populations*

The California Department of Fish and Game needs statistics on the trout population in a Sierra lake to make decisions about fishing limits. Your team has been sent out to take samples of the fish in the lake.

Dragging a large net behind a boat, you catch a good sample of fish. After counting the sample, your team finds the following counts:

Brown trout: 70 fish /14
Rainbow trout: 42 fish 28
Other fish: 56 fish /14

$70 + 42 + 56 = 168$ 42%
25%
33%
100%

1. What is your best guess of the proportions of the different fish populations in the lake, based on the sample? Create a chart or graph to show this.

Student B

Your team then puts identification tags on each of the trout (both brown and rainbow), but not the other fish, and releases all the fish back into the lake.

After allowing the fish to mix with the others in the lake, your team takes another sample with the following results:

Brown trout:
tagged: 15 fish
untagged: 61 fish   ⟩76

Rainbow trout:
tagged: 9 fish
untagged: 36 fish   ⟩45

Other fish (all untagged): 60 fish   60 + 76 + 45 = 181

2. Prepare a report that tells the total number of each kind of fish in the lake. Include charts and/or graphs, as appropriate, and explain how the samples helped you find the total populations.

I added the total amount of tagged and untag fish. Then added them up together. The sampled showed a good number of fishos all together.

Student C

Something's Fishy

This problem gives you the chance to

■ *use the information presented here to try to figure out an estimate of different fish populations*

The California Department of Fish and Game needs statistics on the trout population in a Sierra lake to make decisions about fishing limits. Your team has been sent out to take samples of the fish in the lake.

Dragging a large net behind a boat, you catch a good sample of fish. After counting the sample, your team finds the following counts:

Brown trout: 70 fish
Rainbow trout: 42 fish
Other fish: 56 fish

1. What is your best guess of the proportions of the different fish populations in the lake, based on the sample? Create a chart or graph to show this.

Student C

Your team then puts identification tags on each of the trout (both brown and rainbow), but not the other fish, and releases all the fish back into the lake.

After allowing the fish to mix with the others in the lake, your team takes another sample with the following results:

Brown trout:
tagged: 15 fish
untagged: 61 fish

Rainbow trout:
tagged: 9 fish
untagged: 36 fish

Other fish (all untagged): 60 fish   *Total 181*

2. Prepare a report that tells the total number of each kind of fish in the lake. Include charts and/or graphs, as appropriate, and explain how the samples helped you find the total populations.

Brown 304   Rainbow 180

Brown 2590
2590 Rainbow

There are a total of ≈ 304 Brown Trout. There are ≈ 180 Rainbow Trout. In the second gathering, there were about 25% of Fish tagged in both kind. That means that they represent about ⅓ of the untagged. If you multiply the total by 4 you get the total number of fish

Something's Fishy

This problem gives you the chance to

■ *use the information presented here to try to figure out an estimate of different fish populations*

The California Department of Fish and Game needs statistics on the trout population in a Sierra lake to make decisions about fishing limits. Your team has been sent out to take samples of the fish in the lake.

Dragging a large net behind a boat, you catch a good sample of fish. After counting the sample, your team finds the following counts:

Brown trout: 70 fish
Rainbow trout: 42 fish
Other fish: 56 fish

1. What is your best guess of the proportions of the different fish populations in the lake, based on the sample? Create a chart or graph to show this.

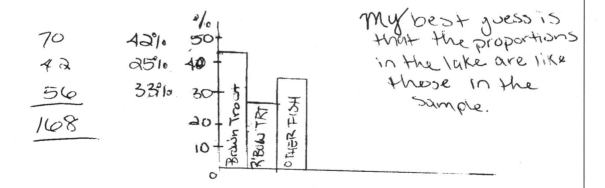

70   42%   50
42   25%   40
56   33%   30
―――
168   20
                   10
                    0

My best guess is that the proportions in the lake are like those in the sample.

Your team then puts identification tags on each of the trout (both brown and rainbow), but not the other fish, and releases all the fish back into the lake.

After allowing the fish to mix with the others in the lake, your team takes another sample with the following results:

Proportions 76/45/60

181

Brown trout:
  tagged: 15 fish $\frac{15}{76}$ = 20% tagged.
  untagged: 61 fish
  76

Rainbow trout:
  tagged: 9 fish   9/45 = 20% tagged   = 42%/25%/33%
  untagged: 36 fish
  45
Other fish (all untagged): 60 fish

2. Prepare a report that tells the total number of each kind of fish in the lake. Include charts and/or graphs, as appropriate, and explain how the samples helped you find the total populations.

The proportions of different fish in the second sample are the same as in the first. So we can assume these are the proportions in the total population of the lake.

Assuming that 20% of all the brown trout are tagged. We know that 70 are tagged (after being caught in the first sample. So there must be 5 × 70 in all or 350.

Also Rainbow trout are 5 × 42 = 210

Other fish are 5 × 56 = 280

Total in lake 840

Miles of Words

See the mathematical ideas implicit in an excerpt from a magazine article.

Make reasonable estimates of two rates.

Combine two rates to get a desired result.

Short Task

Task Description

This task shows an excerpt from a fictitious novel in which it was said that a person uttered 40,000 words during a 200-mile train trip.

Students are asked to show whether this seems like a real possibility. In the process, they are asked to make estimates about the rate of normal speech and the speed of normal trains.

Assumed Mathematical Background

This task involves only a general understanding of percentages.

Core Elements of Performance

- make reasonable estimates of rates for reading and traveling

- use these estimates in conjunction with other data to evaluate the reasonableness of a conclusion concerning the number of words that may be spoken over a given distance

Circumstances

Grouping:	Students complete an individual written response.
Materials:	calculator and stopwatch (optional)
Estimated time:	15 minutes

Miles of Words

This problem gives you the chance to

- *assess the reasonableness that forty thousand words were uttered in a 200-mile train journey*

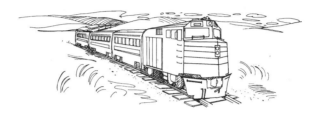

The following excerpt appears on the first page of a fictitious novel:

"Alan sat next to an elderly man during his train ride to Penn Station. The two men sat side by side for the entire two-hundred mile trip. Over that distance Alan uttered about forty thousand words to the stranger. When the train stopped at Penn Station, the two men departed and they never saw each other again."

1. Find a reasonable figure for the rate, in words per minute, of normal spoken language. Show all of your calculations and explain your reasoning.

2. Make an estimate of the average speed of a train in miles per hour.

3. Discuss in detail this statement:
   "Over that distance Alan uttered about forty thousand words . . ."
   Is this statement reasonable? Why or why not? Show all of your calculations and explain your reasoning.

A Sample Solution

1. There are about 60 words in the paragraph from the novel. Reading that excerpt aloud takes about 20 seconds, or 20 ÷ 60 ≈ 0.33 minutes. This is a rate of 60 ÷ 0.33 ≈ 180 words per minute. Any reasonable estimate close to this is acceptable.

2. Trains go fast (greater than 70 mi/hr), but also make stops. An estimate of 60 mi/hr as an average seems reasonable.

3. At a rate of 60 mi/hr, traveling 200 miles takes

   $200 \div 60 = 3\frac{1}{3}$ hours $= (3\frac{1}{3})(60)$ minutes $= 200$ minutes.

   (Quicker: 60 mi/hr = 1 mi/min, so 200 miles requires 200 minutes.)

   At a rate of 180 words per minute, the number of words in 200 minutes is (180)(200) = 36,000 words, assuming the person talked all the time.

   This is not quite 40,000 words. So either the person talked faster, or the train went slower or had multiple stops, or the author exaggerated.

Task

Using this Task

The figuring in question 1 gives $T = \frac{D}{s}$, while the figuring in question 2 gives $N = r\,T$. Combining these gives the result $N = r\left(\frac{D}{s}\right)$. This expresses the number of words in terms of the rate of speed s, the rate of speech r, and the distance D. It can be used to see if the number of words (40,000) mentioned in the article is reasonable.

If it were presented in this straightforward way, the task would be simple and mechanical. But it is not presented in this way. To get to the "heart" of this task, students have to do some meaningful work. They need to make sense of a given written passage where the context is set, and they need to make reasonable estimates of the rate of speed of a train and the rate of normal speech. These estimates will become the "given" rates in the next stage of the task. In carrying out the heart of the task, students need to know (and know how to use) rate relationships such as "distance equals rate times time." They also need to make appropriate unit conversions: the time T they find in question 1 will be in hours, and they will have to convert this to minutes before they can use it in question 2 where the rate is in "words per minute."

Characterizing Performance

This section offers a characterization of student responses and provides indications of the ways in which the students were successful or unsuccessful in engaging with and completing the task. The descriptions are keyed to the *Core Elements of Performance*. Our global descriptions of student work range from "The student needs significant instruction" to "The student's work meets the essential demands of the task." Samples of student work that exemplify these descriptions of performance are included below, accompanied by commentary on central aspects of each student's response. These sample responses are *representative;* they may not mirror the global description of performance in all respects, being weaker in some and stronger in others.

The characterization of student responses for this task is based on these *Core Elements of Performance:*

1. Make reasonable estimates of rates for reading and traveling.
2. Use these estimates in conjunction with other data to evaluate the reasonableness of a conclusion concerning the number of words that may be spoken over a given distance.

Descriptions of Student Work

The student needs significant instruction.

These papers show that the student has understood the requirements of the task and can make a reasonable estimate for speaking or traveling but is unable to begin to use these in solving the problem. Reasoning may be absent or hard to follow.

Student A

This student does not show any reasoning for his answers apart from "I times everything and it still came to way more than 40,000."

The student needs some instruction.

These papers show that the student has understood some of the requirements of the task. The student can make a reasonable estimate for speaking

Task

15

or traveling and can make some progress with solving the problem, but has considerable difficulty in using the concept of rate. Reasoning is clear, but it may be incomplete.

Student B

This student has estimated, reasonably, that a person speaks at approximately 27 words every 15 seconds. She has then incorrectly multiplied 27 by 15 instead of 4 to find the rate of speaking per minute. She therefore writes the answer as 405 words per minute instead of 108. Her reasoning in estimating train speed is flawed and shows confusion about units, rates, and decimals. The final part of her solution shows, however, that she intended (correctly) to multiply the rate of speaking by the time available to obtain an estimate of the number of words spoken.

The student's work needs to be revised.

The student shows an ability to make reasonable estimates of rates for speaking or traveling. The response shows an understanding of the concept of rate, but there may be at most one error in calculation. The reasoning is clear, but it is incomplete and does not indicate how the assumptions may have affected the final result.

Student C

This student has made a reasonable estimate for the train's speed (60–70 mi/hr), and a sensible estimate for the rate of talking (150-170 words/min). He has estimated the time the journey would take as "almost three hours" and has simply stated that in this time only 28,800 words would have been spoken. There is no justification for either of these figures (though they presumably arise from assuming approximate midpoints in his ranges for the rate of speaking and average train speed). The student does not appear to realize that if the fastest estimate of speaking and slowest estimated train speed were taken, then the final word count would be a great deal closer to 40,000.

The student's work meets the essential demands of the task.

The student shows an ability to make reasonable estimates of rates for speaking and traveling. The response shows a clear understanding of the concept of rate and calculations have been planned and carried out correctly, apart from at most, a minor slip in calculation. The reasoning is clear, and if the estimate is said to be unreasonable, the student shows some understanding of how errors in his or her own assumptions may have affected this conclusion.

Student D

This student has explained fully and correctly how he obtained his estimates for the rate of speaking and traveling. He has then gone on to check the reasonableness of the final statement by taking the statement as valid and working backwards. Thus he reasons that if the statement was true, then the man was speaking at 200 words per mile which, at 60mi/hr, is 200 words per minute.

Student E

Student E has made a sensible estimate for both the speaking rate and the average speed of the train. The reasoning is clear, showing how the student has calculated a journey time of 3 hours 36 minutes, has changed this into 216 minutes and has found that this makes it possible for the man to speak 31,104 words. This student also realizes that this result, while appearing to make the estimate seem unreasonable, is inconclusive as it depends on the validity of the initial estimate.

Task

Student A

■ *assess the reasonableness that forty thousand words were uttered in a 200-mile train journey*

The following excerpt appears on the first page of a fictitious novel:

Alan sat next to an elderly man during his train ride to Penn Station. The two men sat side by side for the entire two-hundred mile trip. Over that distance Alan uttered about forty thousand words to the stranger. When the train stopped at Penn Station, the two men departed and they never saw each other again.

1. Find a reasonable figure for the rate, in words per minute, of normal spoken language. Show all of your calculations and explain your reasoning.

     230 words

2. Make an estimate of the average speed of a train in miles per hour.

     80 miles

3. Discuss in detail this statement:
   "Over that distance Alan uttered about forty thousand words . . ."
   Is this statement reasonable? Why or why not? Show all of your calculations and explain your reasoning.

   First I figured out that 230 words are spoken in one minute and that a train goes about 80 miles an hour. I times everything and it still came out to way more than 40 000 words, so I don't think it is reasonable.

The following excerpt appears on the first page of a fictitious novel:

Alan sat next to an elderly man during his train ride to Penn Station. The two men sat side by side for the entire two-hundred mile trip. Over that distance Alan uttered about forty thousand words to the stranger. When the train stopped at Penn Station, the two men departed and they never saw each other again.

1. Find a reasonable figure for the rate, in words per minute, of normal spoken language. Show all of your calculations and explain your reasoning.

   $27/15 \quad 27(4) = 405$ about 405 words/min

2. Make an estimate of the average speed of a train in miles per hour.

   about 150 mph

3. Discuss in detail this statement:
   "Over that distance Alan uttered about forty thousand words . . ."
   Is this statement reasonable? Why or why not? Show all of your calculations and explain your reasoning.

   I assumed that people would talk about 405 words per min (27 up 15s × 4) the I guessed the passenger train would go about 150 mph (150 ÷ 200 = .75 = 1 hr. 15 mins) So, 405 multiplied by 75 minutes = 30.375. Which would be the amount of words spoken for that train under my circumstances therefor the statement is false because the man could only have spoken 30,000 words on that trip. The only way he could have spoken that many words would be if he spoke very fast and the train went slower.

■ *assess the reasonableness that forty thousand words were uttered in a 200-mile train journey*

The following excerpt appears on the first page of a fictitious novel:

Alan sat next to an elderly man during his train ride to Penn Station. The two men sat side by side for the entire two-hundred mile trip. Over that distance Alan uttered about forty thousand words to the stranger. When the train stopped at Penn Station, the two men departed and they never saw each other again.

1. Find a reasonable figure for the rate, in words per minute, of normal spoken language. Show all of your calculations and explain your reasoning.

   between 150 and 170. I timed myself reading it and in one minute I read 160

2. Make an estimate of the average speed of a train in miles per hour.

   60-70 mph

3. Discuss in detail this statement: that in the time he traveled 200 miles he spoke 40,000 words
   "Over that distance Alan uttered about forty thousand words . . ."
   Is this statement reasonable? Why or why not? Show all of your calculations and explain your reasoning. No because 160 words per minute in almost three hours is only 28,800 words.

1. 43
   × 14
   ──
   172

   I talked to myself for 15 seconds. Every word I said was counted. I had spoken 43 words in 15 seconds. Then I multiplied by 4. There are 4, 15 second periods in a minute. This brought me to 172 words a minute.

2. 40,000 ÷ 200 miles = 200 words per mile
   The train was going about (60 mph). He spoke 200 words per minute which comes out to 12,000 word per hour.

3. This means he had to talking at a rate of 200 words per mile.

4. If the train was traveling at 60 and the man was talking at about 200 words a minute then yes it is reasonable.

   200 ÷ 60 = 3.33 hours
   60 × 200 = 12,000 words
   3.33 × 12,000 = 39,960 words

   It took the train aproximitly 3.33 hours to reach its destination. The man spoke 12,000 words in an hour which means he spoke aproximately 39,960 words in the trip.
   Yes

Student E

The following excerpt appears on the first page of a fictitious novel:

Alan sat next to an elderly man during his train ride to Penn Station. The two men sat side by side for the entire two-hundred mile trip. Over that distance Alan uttered about forty thousand words to the stranger. When the train stopped at Penn Station, the two men departed and they never saw each other again.

24 × 6 = 144 words per minute
144 words per minute

1. Find a reasonable figure for the rate, in words per minute, of normal spoken language. Show all of your calculations and explain your reasoning.

   24 words in 10 serounds

2. Make an estimate of the average speed of a train in miles per hour.

   55 miles per hour

3. Discuss in detail this statement:
   "Over that distance Alan uttered about forty thousand words . . ."
   Is this statement reasonable? Why or why not? Show all of your calculations and explain your reasoning.

   Step #2
   144 words per minute
   for
   3 hour 36 minutes

   3 × 60 = 180
   + 36
   216 minutes
   To Penn Station

   Step #1 to Penn Station
   @
   200 miles
   200 miles at 55 miles per hour
   3.6
   55|200 = 3 hours 36 minutes

   To Penn Station
   200 miles
   3 hours 36 minutes

   216 minutes
   216 minutes
   × 144 words per minute
   31,104 words per 200 miles

   No and Yes — No, because by my reasoning he would of only said 31,104 words for the whole trip.

   Yes, because other things may have effected the reasults. Like how fast the man talked.

This glossary defines a number of the terms that are used to describe the *Dimensions of Balance* table that appears in the package Introduction.

Applied power: a task goal—to provide students an opportunity to demonstrate their power over a real-world practical situation, with that as the main criterion for success. This includes choosing mathematical tools appropriately for the problem situation, using them effectively, and interpreting and evaluating the results in relation to the practical needs of the situation. [cf. *illustrative application*]

Checking and evaluating: a mathematical process that involves evaluating the quality of a problem solution in relation to the problem situation (for example, checking calculations; comparing model predictions with data; considering whether a solution is reasonable and appropriate; asking further questions).

Definition of concepts: a task type—such tasks require the clarification of a concept and the generation of a mathematical definition to fit a set of conditions.

Design: a task type that calls for the design, and perhaps construction, of an object (for example, a model building, a scale drawing, a game) together with instructions on how to use the object. The task may include evaluating the results in light of various constraints and desirable features. [cf. *plan*]

Evaluation and recommendation: a task type that calls for collecting and analyzing information bearing on a decision. Students review evidence and make a recommendation based on the evidence. The product is a "consultant" report for a "client."

Exercise: a task type that requires only the application of a learned procedure or a "tool kit" of techniques (for example, adding decimals; solving an equation); the product is simply an answer that is judged for accuracy.

Illustrative application of mathematics: a task goal—to provide the student an opportunity to demonstrate effective use of mathematics in a context outside mathematics. The focus is on the specific piece of mathematics, while the reality and utility of the context as a model of a practical situation are secondary. [cf. *applied power*]

Inferring and drawing conclusions: a mathematical process that involves applying derived results to the original problem situation and interpreting the results in that light.

Modeling and formulating: a mathematical process that involves taking the situation as presented in the task and formulating mathematical statements of the problem to be solved. Working the task involves selecting appropriate representations and relationships to model the problem situation.

Nonroutine problem: a task type that presents an unfamiliar problem situation, one that students are not expected to have analyzed before or have not met regularly in the curriculum. Such problems demand some flexibility of thinking, and adaptation or extension of previous knowledge. They may be situated in a context that students have not encountered in the curriculum; they may involve them in the introduction of concepts and techniques that will be explicitly taught at a later stage; they may involve the discovery of connections among mathematical ideas.

Open-ended: a task structure that requires some questions to be posed by the student. Therefore open-ended tasks often have multiple solutions and may allow for a variety of problem-solving strategies. They provide students with a wide range of possibilities for choosing and making decisions. [cf. *open-middle*]

Open investigation: an open-ended task type that invites exploration of a problem situation with the aim of discovering and establishing facts and relationships. The criteria for evaluating student performance are based on exploring thoroughly, generalizing, justifying, and explaining with clarity and economy.

Open-middle: a task structure in which the question and its answer are well-defined (there is a clear recognizable "answer") but with a variety of strategies or methods for approaching the problem. [cf. *open-ended*]

Plan: a task type that calls for the design of a sequence of activities, or a schedule of events, where time is an essential variable and where the need to organize the efforts of others is implied. [cf. *design*]

Pure mathematics: a task type—one that provides the student an opportunity to demonstrate power over a situation within a mathematics "microworld." This may be an open investigation, a nonroutine problem, or a technical exercise.

Reporting: a mathematical process that involves communicating to a specified "audience" what has been learned about the problem. Components of a successful response include explaining why the results follow from the problem formulation, explaining manipulations of the formalism, and drawing conclusions from the information presented, with some evaluation.

Re-presentation of information: a task type that requires interpretation of information presented in one form and its translation to some different form (for example, write a set of verbal directions that would allow a listener to reproduce a given geometric design; represent the information in a piece of text with a graphic or a symbolic expression).

Review and critique: a task type that involves reflection on curriculum materials (for example, one might review a piece of student work, identify errors, and make suggestions for revision; pose further questions; produce notes on a recently learned topic).

Scaffolding: the degree of detailed step-by-step guidance that a task prompt provides a student.

Task length: the time that should be allowed for students to work on the task. Also important is the length of time students are asked by the task to think independently—the reasoning length. (For a single well-defined question, reasoning length will equal the task length; for a task consisting of many parts, the reasoning length can be much shorter—essentially the time for the longest part.)

Transforming and manipulating: a mathematical process that involves manipulating the mathematical forms in which the problem is expressed, usually with the aim of transforming them into other equivalent forms that represent "solutions" to the problem (for example, dividing one fraction by another, making a geometric construction, solving equations, plotting graphs, finding the derivative of a function).